Balzac's Paris

Balzac's Paris

The City as Human Comedy

Eric Hazan

Translated by David Fernbach

V

VERSO

London • New York

Albertine Translation

This work received support for excellence in publication and translation from Albertine Translation, formerly French Voices, a programme created by Villa Albertine.

This English-language edition first published by Verso 2024
Originally published as *Balʒac, Paris*
© La Fabrique éditions 2018
Translation © David Fernbach 2024

The moral rights of the author and translator have been asserted

1 3 5 7 9 10 8 6 4 2

Verso
UK: 6 Meard Street, London W1F 0EG
US: 388 Atlantic Avenue, Brooklyn, NY 11217
versobooks.com

Verso is the imprint of New Left Books

ISBN-13: 978-1-83976-725-8
ISBN-13: 978-1-83976-727-2 (UK EBK)
ISBN-13: 978-1-83976-728-9 (US EBK)

British Library Cataloguing in Publication Data
A catalogue record for this book is available from the British Library

Library of Congress Cataloging-in-Publication Data

Names: Hazan, Éric, author. | Fernbach, David, translator.
Title: Balzac's Paris : the city as human comedy / Eric Hazan ; translated
   by David Fernbach.
Other titles: Balzac, Paris. English
Description: English-language edition. | London ; New York : Verso, 2024. |
   Includes bibliographical references and index.
Identifiers: LCCN 2023057774 (print) | LCCN 2023057775 (ebook) | ISBN
   9781839767258 (hardback) | ISBN 9781839767289 (e-book)
Subjects: LCSH: Balzac, Honoré de, 1799–1850 – Homes and
   haunts – France – Paris. | Authors, French – 19th century – Biography. |
   Paris (France) – In literature. | Paris (France) – Intellectual life – 19th
   century. | LCGFT: Biographies.
Classification: LCC PQ2184.P3 H3913 2024 (print) | LCC PQ2184.P3 (ebook)
   | DDC 843/.7 [B] – dc23/eng/20240215
LC record available at https://lccn.loc.gov/2023057774
LC ebook record available at https://lccn.loc.gov/2023057775

Typeset in Fournier by Biblichor Ltd, Scotland
Printed and bound by CPI Group (UK) Ltd, Croydon CR0 4YY

Contents

Translations and Acknowledgements

Modern English translations of Balzac's works have been used as follows, and are quoted with page references:

The Black Sheep, trans. Donald Adamson (London: Penguin, 1970)

Cousin Bette, trans. Marion Ayton Crawford (London: Penguin, 1965)

Cousin Pons, trans. Herbert J. Hunt (London: Penguin, 1968)

A Harlot High and Low, trans. Rayner Heppenstall (London: Penguin, 1970)

Lost Illusions, trans. Herbert J. Hunt (London: Penguin 1971)

Old Man Goriot, trans. Catherine McCannon (London: Penguin, 2011)

The Wild Ass's Skin, trans. Herbert J. Hunt (London: Penguin 1977)

'Another Study of Womankind', trans. Jordan Stump; 'Facino Cane', 'Gobseck', and 'Z. Marcas', trans. Linda Asher; and 'The Duchesse de Langeais', trans. Carol Cosman, in *The*

Human Comedy: Selected Stories, ed. Peter Brooks (New York: New York Review Books, 2014).

Other texts are quoted from the Project Gutenberg digital edition of *The Human Comedy*, with location references to the Kindle format. This uses translations by Katherine Prescott Wormeley for the fifty-three-volume edition published by George Barrie (Philadelphia: 1883–97), and by Ellen Marriage (aka James Waring) and Clara Bell for the forty-volume edition published by J. M. Dent (London: 1895–98). Some passages in these have been slightly modified. Orthography has been standardized throughout in the interest of a consistent style.

A comprehensive contents list of *The Human Comedy*, with the original titles alongside those of English translations, is accessible at en.wikipedia.org/wiki/La_Comédie_humaine.

In the footnotes, *Correspondance* I refers to the Pléiade edition (Paris: Gallimard, 2006); and *Correspondance* II–V to the Classiques Garnier edition (Paris: Garnier 1962ff.).

Many thanks to Évelyne Maggiore, my guide in the library of the Maison de Balzac, and to Stéphanie Grégoire and Jean Morisot, whose criticisms and suggestions were essential to the final shape of this manuscript. – Eric Hazan

Why Paris?

For me, Paris is a daughter, a friend, a wife, whose physiognomy always delights me because it is always new to me. I study her at all hours and each time I discover new beauties. She has caprices, she veils herself in rain, cries, and reappears brilliantly, illuminated by a ray of sunshine that hangs diamonds from her roofs. She is majestic here, coquettish there, poor further on; she sleeps, she wakes, she is turbulent or quiet. Ah, my dear city, how sparkling and proud she is on a festive evening, luminous, dancing and quivering.[1]

In his busy life, Balzac wrote many love letters, and, in *The Human Comedy*, he portrayed many female beauties, but he certainly never imagined or met a creature as 'sparkling and proud' as his beloved city.

Like all great loves, Balzac's relationship with Paris had its difficult moments. At times, he felt 'a movement of disgust towards the capital', for 'it is not in mere sport that Paris has been called a hell. Take this phrase for truth,' he writes in his long introduction to *The Girl with the Golden Eyes*.[2] But this text is one of the very few in which Balzac speaks of Paris as a metropolis. He does not use the word, yet the idea is there, that of a great city seen as a totality, 'a vast field constantly stirred by a storm of interests'. More generally, the city to which he addresses his declaration of love consists of an accumulation of details – names, landmarks, streams, gates (how many gates in *The Human Comedy*?) – a city with countless meticulously drawn figures: legal clerks, *grisettes*, journalists, concierges, usurers, salesmen, speculators. Balzac gathered the elements of this Paris by sauntering through it. 'To wander over Paris! What an adorable and delightful existence!' he writes in *Petty Troubles of Married Life*. 'To saunter is a science; it is the gastronomy of the eye. To take a walk is to vegetate; to saunter is to live.'[3] Balzac was certainly one of 'those men of study and thought, of poetry and pleasure, who know how to harvest, by sauntering through Paris, the mass of pleasures floating, at all hours, between its walls'. But when did this man, whose work occupies thirteen volumes in the Pléiade edition as well as seven volumes of correspondence, and who died at the age of fifty-one, get the chance to saunter? Unlike Baudelaire, Apollinaire, or Breton, he had no time to 'lose himself in the crowd'. But, as he walked through the city in his big boots, running between his printers, publishers, coffee merchants, mistresses, and friends, he would probably stop for a moment, struck by a detail that his photographic memory faithfully fixed. 'There are memories for me at every doorway, thoughts at each lamppost. There is no façade constructed, no building pulled down, whose birth or death I have not spied on. I partake in the immense movement of this world as if its soul was mine.'

One could trace an itinerary of *The Human Comedy* that would lead from Issoudun to Guérande, from Alençon to

Fougères, from Sancerre to Besançon. But the epicentre – where 'everything smokes, everything burns, everything shines, everything bubbles, everything flames, evaporates, is extinguished, rekindled, sparkles, fizzles and is consumed' – is Paris.[4]

A Wanderer

During the thirty-five or so years he spent in Paris, Balzac moved house ten times, counting only his official residences, those where he received mail and paid – at times – his rent, and leaving aside any temporary accommodation, holiday addresses, visits to his sister Laure or to friends, and of course his numerous trips to the provinces and abroad. It is not so much that he was restless. After his youth, his moves were almost all made in haste and for the same reason: to escape his creditors – throughout his life he dragged behind him debts incurred at the age of thirty, when his printing business went bankrupt in 1828, aggravating these with spending sprees and unhappy speculations.

In 1813–14, Balzac's father was appointed director of supplies for the First Military Division, and the family left Tours for Paris. Fourteen-year-old Honoré, taken from the Collège de Vendôme where he had spent six years as a boarder, followed the family, which moved to 40 Rue du Temple, at the corner of Rue Pastourelle.[1] This was the first of Balzac's homes in the Marais, the district where he was to spend ten years and where he would set many episodes of *The Human Comedy.*

On arrival, he was sent again to a boarding house, run by a German priest named Ganser on Rue de Thorigny, in what was, until the Revolution, the Hôtel Salé. The building had been nationalized and sold, and the new owner remodelled the interior to serve as an educational establishment.[2]

The young Balzac had to take only a few steps to reach the Collège Charlemagne, on Rue Saint-Antoine, where he entered the fourth year of secondary school. He did not make a great impression there. In January 1814, his awful mother wrote to him:

> I cannot find strong enough expressions to describe the pain you cause me, my dear Honoré . . . The good, estimable M. Ganser told me that you were 32nd in translation . . . I was supposed to send for you at 8 o'clock in the morning, we were to have lunch and dinner together. Your lack of application, your carelessness, your faults condemn me to leave you at the boarding house.[3]

After the fall of the Empire, the schoolboy was removed from Ganser's establishment and placed in another institution, the Hôtel Joyeuse on Rue Saint-Louis.[4] Its director was François Lepître, who was 'fanatically attached to the Bourbons', as Félix de Vandenesse says in *The Lily of the Valley.* (In this we find details of life at Lepître's and the account of another remembered punishment: little Félix got into debt in order to buy extra food, and his mother was furious – 'I was sent back to school in charge of my brother, I lost the dinner at the Frères Provençaux, and was deprived of seeing Talma in *Britannicus*.')[5]

When Balzac senior retired in 1819, the family could no longer afford to live in Paris and moved to Villeparisis. Honoré left college after the rhetoric year and undertook law studies while working for an advocate named Guillonnet-Merville (remembered by him in creating the character of Derville, who makes frequent appearances in *The Human Comedy*, especially as narrator and protagonist in *Gobseck*). But the law bored him. What he wanted was to become a writer and live from his pen. His father agreed to pay him a small allowance, just long enough for him to prove himself.

Honoré then moved into a garret at 9 Rue Lesdiguières. 'A passion for knowledge had flung me into a garret room where I worked nights, and I would spend the day in a nearby library established by Monsieur, the king's brother . . . In fine weather I would at most take a brief stroll on Boulevard Bourdon.'[6] He later evoked this memory in a letter to Madame Hanska: 'I was in an attic on Rue Lesdiguières, leading the life I described in *The Wild Ass's Skin*.'[7] He is alluding to the passage in which Raphaël tells Émile:

> Nothing could be more sordid than this attic with its dirty yellow walls which smelt of poverty and seemed to await a needy scholar. The roof followed a regular downward slope and the badly fitting tiles gave glimpses of the sky. There was room for a bed, a table, one or two chairs, and I could fit my piano beneath the eaves.[8]

After three years in the garret, where he wrote a five-act tragedy in verse (*Cromwell*) and drafted philosophical, poetic, and novelistic texts, Honoré left Rue Lesdiguières and joined his family who had moved to 7 Rue du Roi Doré. He stayed there until the spring of 1824, when, his parents having left for Villeparisis, he divided his time between this distant village – where he had made the all-important acquaintance of Madame de Berny – and a pied-à-terre rented by his parents on Rue de Berry.[9] This was to be his last home in the Marais.

In the summer of 1824, Balzac crossed the Seine and moved to the fifth floor of a building at 2 Rue de Tournon, on the corner with Rue Saint-Sulpice.[10] At this time, he wrote and published works that he himself described as 'commercial literature', under the names of Lord R'Hoone and Horace de Saint-Aubin. But he was not and never would be a good bargainer; the publishers made him wait and paid badly. 'I went out to collect the manuscript of *Wann-Chlore*, for which they offered me, guess what! 600 francs . . . I would rather go and plough the earth with my fingernails than consent to such infamy,' he wrote to Jean Thomassy, a magistrate friend of his.[11]

To earn his keep, Balzac decided to abandon literature and go into business. He became a publisher and, together with the bookseller Urbain Canel, brought out a number of illustrated classics, including Molière and La Fontaine. It was a total failure and Canel went bankrupt. Then, going further up the chain of the book trade, in 1826 Balzac launched himself in the printing business. He bought the assets of a bankrupt company, at 17 Rue des Marais-Saint-Germain, with money borrowed from his father.[12] One more step, and the following year he became a compositor, making what he called 'letters of lead'. All these attempts ended in 1828 with a financial debacle. The various companies were dissolved with enormous liabilities: some 60,000 francs, most of which was owed to his family. Balzac was definitely not gifted for business, though knowledgeable enough to explain in *César Birotteau* the mechanisms leading from speculation to ruin.

In the meantime, beset by various creditors, he left Rue des
Marais in a hurry and rented under the name of Surville, the
husband of his sister Laure, an apartment in a small house at 1
Rue Cassini. During the seven years he spent in the Faubourg
Saint-Jacques – his longest stay in a Paris residence – he enlarged
this space and furnished it luxuriously, and for a time even had
a horse and carriage. But, above all, it was then that he returned
to literature. 'I am going to take up the pen again,' he wrote to
a friend on 1 July 1828, 'and the nimble wing of the raven, or the
goose, must keep me going and help me pay back my mother.'[13]
In Rue Cassini, he wrote and had published a resounding series
of works including *The Chouans* (the first book under his real
name), *A Woman of Thirty*, *Gobseck*, *The Wild Ass's Skin*, *An
Unknown Masterpiece*, *The Country Doctor*, *Eugénie Grandet*,
César Birotteau, *Old Man Goriot* and *The History of the Thirteen*.
In short, it was here that he became the great Balzac. And it was
here, too, that in 1832 he began a correspondence with 'the
Foreigner', a very rich Polish noblewoman, Madame Hanska,
whom he eventually married after many ups and downs.

But literary success did not manage to improve Balzac's financial
situation, which remained disastrous. To escape his creditors, he
left Rue Cassini in March 1835 and retired to an 'unapproachable
cell' at 13 Rue des Batailles in Chaillot, a village just outside
Paris. He thus followed the evolution described in *The Lesser
Bourgeoisie*, 'this progressive movement by which the Parisian
population moves to the heights of the Right Bank of the Seine,
abandoning the Left Bank'. In Rue des Batailles, he hid under
the name of Veuve Durand. As his friend Théophile Gautier
recounts:

The house at 1 Rue Cassini (lithograph by Jean-Jacques Champi)

It was not easy to get into this house, which was better guarded than the Garden of the Hesperides. Two or three passwords were required – these stuck in the mind. To the doorman one would say,

'The plum season has arrived,' and he would let you cross the threshold; to the servant who ran up the stairs at the sound of the bell, you had to say, 'I'm bringing lace from Belgium,' and if you assured the valet that 'Madame Bertrand was in good health,' you would finally be announced.[14]

But an incognito is hard to maintain, and soon the secret of 'widow Durand' was widely discovered. 'Veuve Durand no longer exists,' Balzac wrote to Madame Hanska, 'the poor woman has been killed by petty newspapers who have taken cowardice towards me to the point of betraying a secret which for any man of honour should be sacred.'[15] To escape not only his creditors but also his military obligations, not to mention publishers exasperated at waiting for manuscripts that did not arrive, Balzac moved once again and settled in autumn 1837 in Sèvres, at Les Jardies.[16] The small house he bought there was later enlarged and he carried out major and costly work. In July 1839, he wrote to Madame Hanska: 'I will have about three houses to rent, all overlooking seven acres of enclosed gardens . . . Our railway will be running in a few days and one can board the train from my garden, so that I am closer to the heart of Paris than I have ever been, since for eight sous and in fifteen or twenty minutes I am in Paris.'[17]

However, Balzac had also taken a pied-à-terre in the city, at the heart of the most fashionable district in the late 1830s, the corner of Rue de Richelieu and Boulevard Montmartre, in a building constructed on the former site of Frascati, a famous gambling house. There he rented a small flat from his tailor, Buisson, who had little regard for payment given the publicity represented by such an illustrious client. (Buisson is often mentioned in *The Human Comedy*, particularly as the tailor of Charles

Grandet and the Marquis de Vandenesse. In *The Physiology of Marriage*, we read that 'a suit made by Buisson is enough for a man to become king of a salon'.) But this balance between city and suburb lasted less than two years: a debt incurred with the production of Balzac's play *Vautrin* earned him a bailiff's seizure and forced him to leave Les Jardies in a hurry.

In the autumn of 1840, Balzac found refuge in Passy, another village close to Paris, though almost rural. He rented a small house with a garden on the slope between Rue Basse and Rue du Roc.[18] The lease was in the name of Mme Breugnol, whom Balzac presented to Madame Hanska as a servant but who in fact had a more intimate place in his life, which she occupied for the seven years of his stay in Passy. It was in Passy that Balzac found the magnificent title of *The Human Comedy* and where he wrote, in particular, *The Imaginary Mistress*, *An Historical Mystery*, *Letters of Two Brides*, the various parts of *Lost Illusions*, *A Harlot High and Low*, *Béatrix*, *A Start in Life*, *The Black Sheep*, *The Unconscious Comedians*, and finally the two parts of *Poor Relations* – *Cousin Pons* and *Cousin Bette*. He had every right to write to his friend Zulma Carraud in January 1845: 'You can't imagine what *The Human Comedy* is; it's bigger, literally speaking, than Bourges cathedral architecturally. I've been at it for eight years now, and I need another eight years to finish it.'[19]

From 1845 onwards, however, Balzac had other preoccupations. Hoping that his marriage to Madame Hanska would eventually be concluded, he looked for a new home worthy of her and searched to the west, in Rue du Ranelagh, in Rue de la Tour in Passy, in Batignolles, in the Plaine Monceau . . . Finally, the choice fell on 'a house, situated in the new Beaujon district of

Rue Basse (photograph, anonymous, undated)

Paris, entered from a planned street, provisionally called Rue du
Moulin, consisting of a main building and two courtyards, one
in front of, the other behind the said main building'.[20] The street
was named Rue Fortunée – and from 1850 Rue Balzac. The 'new

Victor Dargaud, *House on Rue Fortunée*, oil on wood, 1889 (Maison de Balzac)

Beaujon district' had recently been developed by subdividing
large plots of land around the Chartreuse Beaujon, a folly built
in the 1780s by a rich financier, Nicolas Beaujon. Thus, the
Champs-Élysées, almost deserted in the days of Balzac's youth,
was now included in the city as far as the part nearest the Arc de
Triomphe. The luxuriously furnished house on Rue Fortunée
was to be Balzac's tenth and last Paris home.

The Street

Most often, in novels set in Paris, the street is a setting, an atmosphere, a background against which the characters move around, meet and have their adventures. The Balzacian street is different: the places where the characters live and evolve are part of their personality; they define them in the same way as their physique, their dress or their psychology. The return of the same streets at different points in *The Human Comedy* reinforces the process first developed in *Old Man Goriot*, with the same characters reappearing from one novel to the next. Some streets are described in moral terms: 'Rue Traversière-Saint-Honoré – is not that a villainous street?', Balzac asks at the beginning of *Ferragus* – and further on: 'Isn't Rue Fromenteau both murderous and low-life?' The action of the novel begins 'at half past eight one evening, in Rue Pagevin, in the days when that street had no wall which did not echo some infamous word'.[1] In contrast to these disreputable places, some streets seem designed to enhance the beauty of women:

This magnificent species prefers to keep to the warmest latitudes, the cleanest longitudes of Paris; you will find her between the 10th and 110th arcade on Rue de Rivoli; along the equator of the Grands Boulevards, from the parallel of the Passage des Panoramas, where the products of the Indies abound, where industry's freshest creations flourish, to the cape of the Madeleine; in those lands least sullied by the bourgeoisie, between the 30th and the 150th house on Rue du Faubourg Saint-Honoré. In the winter, she sojourns on the Terrace des Feuillants, in the Jardin des Tuileries, and not on the asphalt sidewalk that adjoins it.[2]

The streets characterized in this way had certain common features, one of which is announced on the very first page of *Old Man Goriot*: 'that illustrious valley of endlessly crumbling stucco and black, mud-clogged gutters'. Paris, a city of mud – that was not a new observation: it can be found in Nicolas Boileau's *Embarras de Paris*, and in Louis-Sébastien Mercier's *Tableau de Paris*. 'What gambols does not one make in undertaking to go from the Faubourg Saint-Jacques to dine in the Faubourg Saint-Honoré, defending oneself from horse droppings and dripping roofs! Piles of mud, a slippery roadway, greasy axles – what a lot of pitfalls to avoid!'[3] At the beginning of *Les Mystères de Paris*, 'a stream of blackish water' flows through 'the muddy cobblestones' in front of Notre-Dame.[4] And mud is found a little later in Baudelaire: 'Oh ends of autumn, winters, springtimes drenched in mud'; or 'Just now, as I raced across the street, stomping in the mud . . .'[5]

If mud was omnipresent in Paris at the time of Balzac, it was because pavements were still rare (the first ones, in Rue de l'Odéon, date from 1817), roads were rarely asphalted and drainage was precarious.[6] In the old town centre, the streets were drained more or less poorly by a central stream – for example, Rue de Normandie in the Marais, where Cousin Pons lives, is 'one of those ancient streets with a runnel down the middle; the municipal authorities have installed no street fountain in it, and a noisome gutter sluggishly carried off all the household slops which filter through the cobbles and produce the kind of sludge peculiar to Paris'.[7] Similarly, there is the Rue des Cinq-Diamants, in Les Halles, where Birotteau sets up his protégé, the young Popinot, as a hardware merchant: 'That bad-smelling Rue des Cinq-Diamants, without sun and without air, frightens me. The gutter is always blue or green or black.' Often the water stagnates, as in Rue du Tourniquet-Saint-Jean, where 'in rainy weather the gutter water was soon deep at the foot of the old houses, sweeping down with it the dust and refuse deposited at the corner-stones by the residents'. Or it trickles down, as in Rue du Fouarre where Judge Popinot lived, 'a street which is always damp, and where the gutter carries to the Seine the blackened waters from some dye-works'.[8]

For poor young people forced to walk, the mud was a scourge. The student Rastignac sometimes returned to the Vauquer boarding house in the early hours of the morning from a ball, 'his silk stockings splashed with mud and his pumps trodden out of shape'. This was not serious, but when he had to walk from Montagne Sainte-Geneviève to Rue du Helder where he hoped to be received by Madame de Restaud, despite taking 'a thousand precautions to avoid being spattered with mud . . . he had to have his boots polished and trousers brushed at the Palais-Royal'.[9]

The white silk stockings that were part of the dandy's uniform were particularly vulnerable to mud. Théodore de Sommervieux, a young painter returning from Rome, gazed nightly at the front of the house of The Cat and Racket in Rue Saint-Denis, hoping to see Augustine, that 'exiled angel reminiscent of heaven'. 'His coat, folded after the manner of an antique drapery, showed a smart pair of shoes, all the more remarkable in the midst of the Parisian mud, because he wore white silk stockings, on which the splash stains betrayed his impatience.'[10] That didn't matter, as he was alone in the deserted street. But in *The Wild Ass's Skin*, Raphaël confides to Blondet:

> My happiness and my love depended on a spatter of dirt on my one and only white waistcoat. To have to give up all idea of seeing her if my clothes were muddied or if I got wet! To be without five sous to pay a shoeblack to remove the smallest spot of mud on my boots! My passion had increased with all these unsuspected tortures, which to an irritable man were tremendous.[11]

The domain of mud was not limited to the street. The floor of the Glazed Gallery of the Palais-Royal, where

> Chevet laid the foundations of his fortune . . . was the natural soil of Paris, reinforced by the adventitious dirt brought in on the boots and shoes of passers-by. In all seasons, one's feet stumbled against mounds and depressions of caked mud; the shopkeepers were constantly sweeping them up, but newcomers had to acquire the knack of walking across them.[12]

In *A Harlot High and Low*, the sinister Asie wants to get a message to Carlos Herrera/Vautrin, who is being taken to the Palais de Justice in a *panier à salade* (salad basket – Balzac's term).[13] To this end, she organizes a huge traffic jam with her cart in Arcade Saint-Jean, the passageway that connects Rue du Martroi with the square through the Hôtel de Ville.[14]

The two massive walls of Arcade Saint-Jean were clothed up to a
height of six feet with a permanent mantle of mud produced by
splashes from the gutter; for in those days the only thing that
protected passers-by from the incessant passing of carriages and
what were called cart-kicks was a succession of posts long ago
smashed by the hubs and pipe-boxes of wheels.[15]

Gobseck, the master usurer in *The Human Comedy*, confides to
Derville: 'I like to leave mud on a rich man's carpet; it is not
petty spite, I like to make them feel a touch of the claws of
Necessity.'[16] Here, the mud takes on a moral value. When the
young Rastignac says to Vautrin in disgust: 'Why, then, this
Paris of yours is a dunghill', the irony of Vautrin's reply would
not have displeased Gobseck: 'And a funny old dunghill it is
too . . . A man in a carriage who gets his hands dirty is honest,
a man who walks and gets his feet dirty is a rogue.'[17]

How do those who can afford not to get dirty on foot get
around Paris? The high aristocracy have their carriages bearing
the coat of arms of their lineage, so that they are identified as they
pass and their presence, even empty, is like a visiting card. When
the Duchesse de Langeais leaves her carriage for a whole morning in front of the Marquis de Montriveau's hotel, 'on Rue de
Seine, a few steps from the Chamber of Peers', a scandal is bound
to occur: 'Instantly the news was telegraphed to all the coteries
in the Faubourg Saint-Germain, reaching the Élysée-Bourbon
palace, becoming the news of the day, the subject of all conver-
sations from noon to evening.'[18] At the end of *Old Man Goriot*, we
see behind the miserable convoy of the deceased, from Saint-
Étienne-du-Mont to Père-Lachaise, 'two emblazoned but empty
carriages, belonging to the Comte de Restaud and the Baron de
Nucingen'. These characters did not want to attend the burial of

their wives' father, but they did what was necessary to ensure that it could not be said that they were not there.

As for the fashionable young people, they ride in a tilbury or gig, a light cabriolet drawn by a single horse. Balzac himself had, as we have seen, a tilbury and a horse. And Lucien de Rubempré, in his heyday, had 'three fine horses in his stable, a brougham for the evening, a cabriolet and a gig for the daytime'.[19] Elegant young women have, like Madame Schontz in *Béatrix*, 'a small barouche and a low two-horse carriage'.

To deal with the unexpected, one could hail a fiacre, or take one of the many omnibuses that circulated in Paris; heavy carriages pulled by four horses abreast, which could carry up to twenty passengers.[20] The characters in *The Human Comedy*, while often using fiacres, do not take public transport – nor did Balzac, who was a tireless walker, crossing Paris in all directions from one print shop to another, or fetching the coffees required for his blend, which 'consisted of three kinds of beans: bourbon, martinique and mocha. He bought the bourbon in Rue du Mont-Blanc; the martinique in Rue des Vieilles-Audriettes, from a grocer who has not forgotten his glorious customer; the mocha in Rue de l'Université, Faubourg Saint-Germain.'[21]

At the beginning of *Ferragus*, we read:

> Oh Paris! He who has not admired your gloomy passages, your gleams and flashes of light, your deep and silent cul-de-sacs, who has not listened to your murmurings between midnight and two in the morning, knows nothing as yet of your true poesy, nor your great and fantastic contrasts.[22]

In Balzac's work, the city at night is dark and even black, despite the introduction of modern street lighting in the first half of the century. In the stories of *The Human Comedy* that take place towards the end of the Empire and under the Restoration, artificial light was provided by the *réverbères* that had replaced the old tallow candle lanterns of Louis XV's reign. These were also lanterns, but fitted with an oil lamp and a polished copper reflector which gave them greater range and intensity. They were suspended from a system of ropes and pulleys stretched between the houses, which allowed them to be lowered while the lamplighter cut the wick, filled the oil tank, cleaned the reflector and lit the lantern. (During the Revolution, to put the aristocrats 'to the lantern' [*à la lanterne*] meant to hang them using the ropes and pulleys of the lanterns – not to hang the rope from a fixed lampstand, which did not exist.) Balzac never misses an opportunity to speak out against the 'hideous street-lamps'. On Rue de Langlade, where the beautiful Esther lives at the beginning of *A Harlot High and Low*, 'coming from the bright lights of Rue Saint-Honoré, Rue Neuve des Petits Champs and Rue de Richelieu . . . thick shadow succeeds upon a torrent of gaslight. At wide intervals, a pale street-lamp casts its smoky and uncertain gleam, not seen at all in some of the blind alleys.'[23]

The 'torrent of gaslight' refers to the slow spread of gas lighting, after its first appearance in 1817 in the Passage des Panoramas, throughout the city under the July Monarchy. In Balzac's time it was limited to the upper-class districts, and the wealthiest even had gas in their homes. In *Cousin Bette*, Josépha, the beautiful singer, lives on Rue de la Ville-l'Évêque, in 'one of those pretty modern houses with double doors where, as soon as the gas lantern is lit, luxury becomes apparent'. The Left Bank and the working-class districts remained in the shadow of the *réverbères*.[24] But, even in those parts of *The Human Comedy* set in the 1840s – by which time gas had largely prevailed – the night-time exterior remains mainly in darkness. Illuminated café terraces were to come later, and the fragile light of the *réverbères* still appears in Baudelaire's *Evening Twilight*: 'Among the gas flames worried by the wind / Prostitution catches alight in the streets.'

Balzac was not particularly enthusiastic about gas, nor about the other technical innovations of the time. He was more atten-tive to destruction than to innovation. Although he repeatedly details the advantages of the railway in his correspondence, this mode of transport is only present in *The Human Comedy* as a sign of the times, in the opening lines of *A Start in Life*: 'Railroads, in a future not far distant, must force certain industries to dis-appear forever, and modify several others, more especially those relating to the different modes of transportation in use around Paris.'[25] But there is no mention of the stations built at the time, and we do not see any of the characters taking the train: when they leave Paris, it is by stagecoach or in one of the *coucous* that leave for the north from the Faubourg Saint-Denis.

At the beginning of *The Lesser Bourgeoisie*, we read: 'Alas! Old Paris is disappearing with frightening rapidity.' And in 1845, Balzac published a short text, 'Ce qui disparaît de Paris':

> The pillars of Les Halles will have disappeared in a few days, and old Paris will exist only in the works of novelists brave enough to describe faithfully the last vestiges of the architecture of our fathers; for the serious historian takes little account of these things.[26]

The pillars of Les Halles were massive stone arches under which for centuries merchants had protected their stalls from rain and

Charles Marville, *Les Halles Pillars*, Rue de la Tonnellerie, c. 1866

mud. 'To the shame of the city, a filthy modern building in yellow plaster was constructed there, removing the pillars.' This destruction, some twenty years before Baltard, was the first in a series of disasters for the Halles district, a series that is not yet over.

But Balzac was not a militant like his friend Victor Hugo, who wrote in 1832: 'Whatever the rights of ownership, the destruction of a historic building must not be permitted these despicable speculators whose interest blinds them to their honour; wretched men, and so imbecilic that they do not even understand that they are barbarians!'[27] Balzac's own tone is rather melancholy:

> In a few years, the lamplighter, who slept during the day, his family having no other home than the contractor's shop, and walked busily all day, the wife cleaning the panes, the husband inserting oil, the children rubbing the reflectors with dirty cloths; who spent the day preparing for the night, and spent the night turning off and

on the light according to the whims of the moon – this family coated in oil will be entirely lost.

Likewise the clothes mender 'housed like Diogenes in a barrel topped by a niche for a statue made of hoops and waxed cloth', and the red umbrellas 'under the shelter of which fruit trees blossomed', and 'the street cleaner's saddle, the stalls metamorphosed into long boards rolling on two old wheels', and 'the shellfish seller, the paper-monger, the fruit growers and the old clothes dealers, and the butchers, and the whole world of small businesses'. The conclusion is almost topical:

> One may ask, without insulting His Royal Highness Political Economy, whether the greatness of a nation depends on the fact that a pound of sausages is delivered to you on carved Carrara marble, or that the fat man is better housed than those who live from him! Our false Parisian splendours have produced the miseries of the provinces and the faubourgs. The victims are in Lyon and are called *canuts*. Every industry has its *canuts*.

For the oldest of present-day readers, there is something disturbing about this passage. They can remember the horse-drawn milk trucks – large wooden trays on rubber-tyred wheels, carrying the tin churns in which one-litre measures were plunged, as well as the cylindrical hairdresser's signs rotating in alternate colours, the two-wheeled fruit-and-vegetable carts with a long handle for balance at a standstill, the gilded horse heads in the windows of the specialist butcher's shops. They have the right to wonder about what will be left of today's Paris to fuel a new stanza of the recurrent complaint in fifty years' time: 'Old Paris is no more', wrote Baudelaire, 'the form of a city / Changes more quickly, alas! than the human heart.'

Quarters

Of the constellation of quarters in which *The Human Comedy* takes place, some are large, such as the Marais or the Faubourg Saint-Marceau; others, such as Little Poland or Saint-Georges, are made up of just a few intersecting streets. Whatever they are, however, Balzac does not draw fixed boundary lines, specifying either their geographical limits or their architectural features. To characterize them, he chooses metonymic details, such as the house on Rue des Grès where Gobseck lives, emblematic of the miserable Latin Quarter: 'The house has no courtyard, and it is damp and gloomy. The building is divided into a series of cell-like rooms of equal size; their only light comes from the street-front windows, and their only exit is onto a single long corridor lit by dim transoms [*jours de souffrance*]. The claustral arrangement indicates that the building was once part of a convent.'[1] In contrast to this, the mansion built by Count Laginski, a Polish nobleman exiled in Paris, on Rue de la Pépinière, 'built of stone decorated like a melon', represents the luxury and bad taste of the *nouveaux riches* established west of the Chaussée-d'Antin:

A mixture of styles is confusedly employed. As there is no longer a real court or nobility to give the tone, there is no harmony in the production of art . . . Propose to an architect to build upon the garden at the back of an old mansion, and he will run you up a little Louvre overloaded with ornament. He will manage to get in a courtyard, stables, and, if you care for it, a garden. Inside the house he will accommodate a quantity of little rooms and passages. He is so clever in deceiving the eye that you think you have plenty of space; but it is only a nest of small rooms, after all, in which a ducal family has to turn itself about in the space that its own bake-house formerly occupied.[2]

In his foreword to *The Human Comedy*, Balzac writes: 'Thus the work to be done had to have a triple form: men, women and things, that is to say, people and the material representation

De Marsay (Bertall, Édition Furne)

they give of their thoughts; finally, man and life.' It is people as much as things that define Parisian quarters in *The Human Comedy*.

The notion of quarter is given its meaning by the social status of its inhabitants. De Marsay, rich and powerful – he will end up as prime minister – lives in the Faubourg Saint-Germain and has a life of pleasure with his friends in the Palais-Royal and on the boulevards. He need never venture into the Marais or the Latin Quarter. The perfumer César Birotteau rarely leaves the commercial district around Rue Saint-Honoré between Place Vendôme and Les Halles. The Saint-Georges quarter is that of the pretty and witty *lorettes*, named after the church recently built at the end of the Chaussée-d'Antin, the district of the rich and the bankers. At the beginning of *Old Man Goriot*, the young and still naïve Rastignac tries to see the Comtesse de Restaud again, after dancing with her a few days before, but he is turned away on Rue du Helder, where Maxime de Trailles, one of the 'princes of Bohemia', reigns 'morganatically'. To console himself for this humiliation, he has himself taken to the mansion of his cousin, Madame de Bauséant, on Rue de Grenelle, but here too the poor student has a bad time, for the cousin has just learned that her lover is about to get married. In these dazzling pages, Balzac makes us sense the gap between Rue du Helder and Rue de Grenelle, the Chaussée-d'Antin and the Faubourg Saint-Germain, the money district and the aristocratic nobility, without spelling this out.

In *The Human Comedy*, people sometimes abandon their original quarter for another, often distant and alien to their condition. It is the back-and-forth movement of the 'social escalator' that causes such migrations. When it goes up, we see the young

Anselme Popinot (nephew of Judge Popinot), once he had become a count, a peer of France, and a minister after the revolution of 1830, move from Rue des Cinq-Diamants, where he had set up his hardware shop, to Rue Basse-du-Rempart.[3] When it goes down, Honorine, an unfaithful wife, leaves her husband's mansion on Rue Payenne, whose peristyle 'was of a magnificence worthy of Versailles', for a small pavilion on Rue Saint-Maur where you 'could be a hundred leagues from Paris'. (It must be said that her husband kept her without her knowledge, having not lost the hope of recovering her.)[4]

Although precise about the denizens of each quarter, Balzac does not engage in what we would nowadays call 'sociological' surveys or descriptions. Just as he does not describe the general architecture of a quarter, so he does not identify human groups that are linked by origin or occupation. To evoke certain groups, he sometimes uses an original and magnificent procedure, a long list of proper names. In the Faubourg Saint-Germain, for example:

> The Portuguese noblewoman, who cared very little for going out, was much of the time surrounded by her neighbours the Chaulieus, the Navarreins, the Lenoncourts. Frequently the pretty Baroness Macumer (*née* Chaulieu), the Duchesse de Maufrigneuse, Madame d'Espard, Madame de Camps, Mademoiselle des Touches, allied to the Brittany Grandlieus, came to visit her, on their way to a ball or returning from the Opéra. The Vicomte de Grandlieu, the Duc de Rhétoré, the Marquis de Chaulieu, who would one day be Duc de Lenoncourt-Chaulieu, his wife, Madeleine de Mortsauf, granddaughter of the Duc de Lenoncourt, the Marquis d'Ajuda-Pinto, Prince Blamont-Chauvry, the Marquis de Beauséant, the Vidame de Pamiers, the Vandenesses, old Prince Cadignan and his son the Duc de Maufrigneuse, came

regularly to this grandiose drawing-room in which one breathed the air of the Court.[5]

Or among the roués, Victurnien, the naïf protagonist of *The Collection of Antiquities*,

> fell in with a set of roués, with de Marsay, de Ronquerolles, Maxime de Trailles, des Lupeaux, Rastignac, Ajuda-Pinto, Beaudenord, de la Roche-Hugon, de Manerville, and the Vandenesses, whom he met wherever he went . . . to the Marquise d'Espard's, to the Duchesses de Grandlieu, de Carigliano and de Chaulieu, to the Marquises d'Aiglemont and de Listomère, to Mme. de Sérisy's, to the Opéra, to the embassies and elsewhere.[6]

If these lists read like poems, it is because they are rhythmic and composed of names chosen for their suggestive power. Balzac spent a lot of time on these, as Gozlan recounts. 'I am not alone,' he said, 'in believing in this marvellous alliance of the name and the man who adorns himself with it like a talisman,' and he dragged Gozlan all over Paris in search of a name 'for an extraordinary man, a name proportionate to his destiny, a name that explains him, that paints him, that announces him as a cannon announces itself from afar and says, "I'm called a cannon."' They walked to Rue de la Jussienne, where

> Balzac, after raising his gaze above a poorly marked gate in the wall, an oblong, narrow, dilapidated gate opening into a damp and dark alley, suddenly changed his tone and, with a shiver that passed from his arm to mine, uttered a cry and said: 'There! There! Read it, read it!' His voice broke with emotion. And I saw the name MARCAS.[7]

In Proust, a great reader of Balzac, we find the same attention to names. If we compare the surnames in his youthful writings with those of the *Recherche*, we see the banal – Jean Santeuil – give way to the perfect: the Verdurins, Swann, Bergotte, Charlus . . . And those who suffer from a double addiction, to *The Human Comedy* and to *La Recherche du temps perdu*, can dream that Madame de Listomère is the great-aunt of Madame de Villeparisis and that the Duc de Navarreins has links with the Guermantes through his wife.

The technique is one of evoking without describing; Balzac uses similar listings for places, for example the Observatoire crossroads:

the space which lies between the south entrance of the Luxembourg and the north entrance of the Observatoire – a space without a name, the neutral space of Paris. There, Paris is no longer; and there, Paris still lingers. The spot is a mingling of street, square, boulevard, fortification, garden, avenue, high-road, province, and metropolis; certainly, all of that is to be found there, and yet the place is nothing of all that – it is a desert. Around this spot without a name stand the Enfants-Trouvés [foundling hospital], the Bourbe, the Cochin hospital, the Capucines, the hospital of La Rochefoucauld, the Sourds-Muets [asylum for the deaf and dumb], the hospital of Val-de-Grâce; in short, all the vices and all the misfortunes of Paris find their asylum there. And (that nothing may lack in this philanthropic centre) Science there studies the tides and longitudes, Monsieur de Chateaubriand has erected the Marie-Thérèse infirmary, and the Carmelites have founded a convent. The great events of life are represented by bells which ring incessantly through this desert – for the mother giving birth, for the babe that is born, for the vice that succumbs, for the toiler who dies, for the virgin who prays, for the old man shaking with cold, for genius self-deluded. And a few steps off is the cemetery of

Montparnasse, where, hour after hour, the sorry funerals of the Faubourg Saint-Marceau wend their way.[8]

The Left Bank

Despite its old churches and respectable buildings, the Left Bank has changed more profoundly since Balzac's time than the Right Bank. The cuttings that organize it today – Boulevard Saint-Germain, Rue des Écoles, Boulevard Saint-Michel, Rue Soufflot extended to the Luxembourg – often make it difficult to follow the itineraries of *The Human Comedy*, especially since this bank has become the homogeneous carousel of a luxury supermarket, whereas at the beginning of the nineteenth century it was broken up into different small quarters.

Montagne Sainte-Geneviève

The Left Bank accounted for three of the twelve arrondissements of Paris at the time, surrounded by the Wall of the Farmers-General. The only arrondissement explicitly mentioned in *The Human Comedy* is the last one, the XIIth, whose territory corresponds roughly to that of Montagne Sainte-Geneviève and its two slopes, the Latin Quarter descending from the Panthéon towards the Seine, and Faubourg Saint-Marceau to the south, stretching along Rue Mouffetard to the Barrière d'Italie. At the beginning of *The Commission in Lunacy*, Bianchon, who has become a famous doctor, visits his uncle, the judge Popinot, who lives behind Saint-Julien-le-Pauvre in Rue du Fouarre,

> one of the dirtiest streets in the XIIth arrondissement, the poorest district in Paris, the one in which two-thirds of the population

lacks wood in winter, the one that throws the most children into the Enfants-Trouvés, the most sick people to the Hôtel-Dieu, the most rag-pickers to the street corners, the most decrepit old people along the walls where the sun shines, the most unemployed workers into the squares, the most criminals to the police courts.[9]

At this time, the Latin Quarter was as poor as the Faubourg Saint-Marceau.

The Pension Vauquer, where so many characters meet and so many destinies are entwined, lies on the border between the two and constitutes a nerve centre in *The Human Comedy*. Moreover, it is from *Old Man Goriot* onwards that Balzac starts to transfer his heroes, companions, and places from one book to the next, thus giving the work the unity of a cathedral, as he put it. The Pension Vauquer is precisely located on Rue Neuve-Sainte-Geneviève, 'just where the ground shelves into Rue de l'Arbalète so sharply and inconveniently that horses rarely go up or down it', a detail grasped only by those who walk a lot in the city.[10] As Walter Benjamin, another great Parisian pedestrian, wrote, 'Balzac has secured the mythic constitution to his world through precise topographic contours.'[11]

Students, aspiring writers, journalists, artists, dreamy philosophers: in *The Human Comedy* the Latin Quarter is the territory of youth. The older characters who live there are not peaceful bourgeois as in the Marais, but rather marginal figures, such as Gobseck the usurer on Rue des Grès, or Vautrin, the escaped convict, in the Pension Vauquer. And even Monsieur de Restaud, despite being a marquis, finds himself in an unusual position, not so much because he lives on Rue de la Montagne-Sainte-Geneviève,

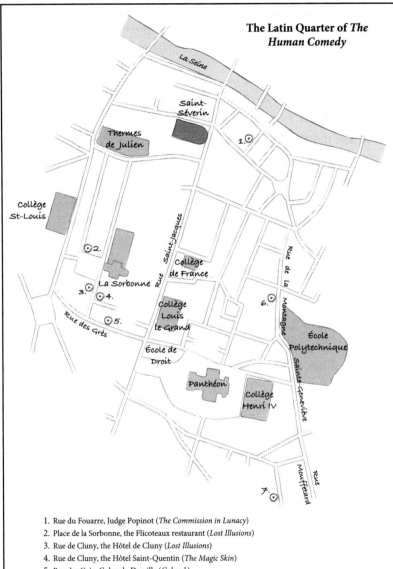

The Latin Quarter of *The Human Comedy*

La Seine

Saint-Séverin

Thermes de Julien

1.

Collège St-Louis

2.

Rue Saint-Jacques

La Sorbonne

Collège de France

3.

4.

5.

Rue des Grès

Collège Louis le Grand

6.

Rue de la Montagne Sainte-Geneviève

École Polytechnique

École de Droit

Panthéon

Collège Henri IV

7.

Rue Mouffetard

1. Rue du Fouarre, Judge Popinot (*The Commission in Lunacy*)
2. Place de la Sorbonne, the Flicoteaux restaurant (*Lost Illusions*)
3. Rue de Cluny, the Hôtel de Cluny (*Lost Illusions*)
4. Rue de Cluny, the Hôtel Saint-Quentin (*The Magic Skin*)
5. Rue des Grès, Gobseck, Derville (*Gobseck*)
6. Rue de la Montagne-Sainte-Geneviève, the Marquis de Restaud (*The Commission in Lunacy*)
7. Rue Neuve-Sainte-Geneviève (Tournefort), the Vauquer boarding house (*Old Man Goriot*)

on the third floor of 'one of those ancient monuments built of dressed stone, which did not lack a certain richness of architecture', but because his wife seeks to have him 'certified' on the grounds of insanity.[12]

Among the students who inhabit the streets of the Latin Quarter (all young men, there were no female students at the time), there are three whom Balzac will make important characters. Derville, who lived on Rue des Grès at the beginning, studied law while working for a notary – like Balzac when he lived with his parents on Rue du Temple. His rigorous and honest figure appears often in *The Human Comedy*: he is the solicitor of César Birotteau, Old Man Goriot and Félix de Vandenesse, the champion of Colonel Chabert, and also the narrator of *Gobseck*. Two other students live in the Pension Vauquer, Horace Bianchon and Eugène de Rastignac. The former is an intern at the Cochin Hospital. The way he treats the dying Goriot – applying mustard poultices and mugwort, changing his sheets and his shirt, diagnosing his symptoms, and enlisting the whole faculty for him – gives us a glimpse of what he was to become: a learned, disinterested doctor, devoted to the poor as well as the rich, the most famous of his generation. Present in many episodes of *The Human Comedy*, he is one of the very few male characters described by Balzac after his own heart – along with D'Arthez, the writer with whom the glorious Duchesse de Maufrigneuse will retire after a turbulent life, becoming the Princesse de Cadignan. Bianchon is a great practitioner, and morally impeccable, but he is neither austere nor boring: he knows how to laugh and have fun, and often takes part in the parties and dinners of *The Human Comedy* in the company of pretty and not too shy women. He can even write, and we see him reworking Lucien de Rubempré's novel, *The Archer of Charles the Ninth*: 'His portraits, somewhat woolly in outline, had been brought into strong and colourful relief; all of them were linked up with the interesting phenomena of human life by means of physiological comments, due no doubt to Bianchon, expressed with subtlety and infusing life into them.'[13] He was also a good storyteller: in *Another Study of Womankind*, he tells the terrifying story of La Grande Bretèche, which Edgar Poe drew on for *The Cask of Amontillado* (1846). Legend has it that, on his deathbed, Balzac asked for Bianchon to be brought in.

For Rastignac, *Old Man Goriot* is a *Bildungsroman*. When he arrives from his native Charente to study law, he is naïve and charming; he understands nothing of the world. But he learns quickly, and by the end of the book he is the lover of Delphine de Nucingen, housed by her on the elegant Rue d'Artois.[14] Enlightened by his association with the nobility, he is ready to become a lion and casts his challenge to Paris from the heights of Père-Lachaise: 'Now let us fight it out!' He will end up as a peer of France and a minister.

Law and medicine, the disciplines that led to a profession at the time, are the only higher studies mentioned in *The Human Comedy* – and even then, we never attend a lecture, enter an amphitheatre, or catch a glimpse of the actual academic life of student youth. Nowhere, unless I am mistaken, is there any mention of the then famous lectures of François Guizot or Victor Cousin in the faculty of letters, and the Sorbonne is just one topographical landmark among others. The academic world is absent from *The Human Comedy* – perhaps it was not as important as it has since become.

Rastignac at Père-Lachaise (Laisné, Édition Furne)

Balzac never lived in the Latin Quarter, but he remembered enough attics to know how penniless youths were housed. Those who could not afford a boarding house or were averse to the idea of collective living could choose a hotel. At the beginning of 'A Great Man in Embyro', Lucien de Rubempré, 'discharged, disowned, repudiated' by Madame de Bargeton, with whom he had come from Angoulême, finds himself with 'three hundred and sixty francs out of the two thousand francs he had brought to Paris'. He hurries to 'the Latin Quarter, recommended to him by David [his brother-in-law, a printer] as being cheap. After a long search he at last found, on Rue de Cluny near the Sorbonne, a wretched lodging-house with furnished rooms for the price he was willing to pay.'[15] To his sister Eve, Lucien wrote,

> After living in an elegant quarter, I am now at the Hôtel de Cluny in Rue de Cluny, in one of the poorest and dingiest back-streets in Paris, squeezed between three churches and the ancient buildings of the Sorbonne. I have taken a furnished room on the fourth floor, a very bare and dirty one – but I still have to pay fifteen francs a month for it.[16]

Lucien de Rubempré
(Nanteuil, Édition Furne)

When an old publisher named Doguereau comes round to buy
his novel:

> He was resolved to pay one thousand francs for sole rights in *The
> Archer of Charles the Ninth*, and to bind Lucien by a contract for
> several other works. But when the old fox saw the building he had
> second thoughts. 'A young man in such a lodging,' he told himself,
> 'has modest tastes; he's in love with study and toil. I need only pay
> him eight hundred francs.'

Finally, he offers to buy the manuscript for four hundred francs,
which Lucien haughtily refuses: 'Monsieur, I would rather burn it!'[17]

It is on the same street, in *The Wild Ass's Skin*, that Raphaël,
looking for a quiet place for his research, finds a hotel corre-
sponding to his means:

> One evening, on my way back from the Estrapade, I was passing
> through Rue des Cordiers on my way home. At the corner of Rue
> de Cluny, I saw a young girl of about fourteen playing with a hoop
> along with her friends, and her laughter and mischief amused the
> neighbours . . . It was a delightful scene. Seeking the cause of this
> bonhomie in the middle of Paris, I noticed that the street did not
> lead to anything and cannot have been very busy. Recalling J.-J.
> Rousseau's stay in this place, I found the Hôtel Saint-Quentin; its
> state of dilapidation made me hope to find a cheap lodging there,
> and I decided to visit it.[18]

The proprietor 'led the way up to the attic where she showed me
a room that looked out over the roofs and upon the courtyards
of neighbouring houses from whose windows long poles
protruded with clothes drying'.[19]

Among those living in hotels in the Latin Quarter, the
most unfortunate is neither a student nor even very young. In

the short story that bears his name, Z. Marcas lives on Rue Corneille

> in a hotel intended entirely for students, one of those hotels where the staircase turns at the back, lit first by the street, then by dim lights [*jours de souffrance*], and finally by a window. There were forty rooms, furnished in the way rooms for students are furnished. What more does youth need than what was there: a bed, some chairs, a chest of drawers, a mirror and a table?

The narrator, a law student, and his roommate, a medical student, eventually meet their next-door neighbour, Z. Marcas, an extremely silent man who spends his time copying court documents for a living. 'His closet stood open, revealing just two shirts, a white cravat, and a razor. The straight razor made me shudder. A mirror worth perhaps a few francs hung by the window. The man's simple, spare gestures had a kind of primitive nobility.'[20] Marcas tells the two young rogues about the setbacks in journalism and politics that brought him to Rue Corneille: 'The intestinal disease of the country had passed into its bowels.' His remarks echo strangely in our ears today:

> Youth is going to explode like the boiler of a steam engine. Youth has no outlet in France; it is gathering an avalanche of unrecognized abilities, of legitimate and unsatisfied ambitions . . . What shock will come and shake loose these masses I do not know, but they will surge forward into the current situation and overrun it.[21]

In the last lines, we learn that the day after telling his story, the narrator embarked on a brig in Le Havre to seek his fortune in the Malaysian islands. Of the population of the Latin Quarter, the only happy ones are those who leave.

To feed themselves, these penniless young people have an address, the Flicoteaux restaurant. 'At that period this celebrated establishment consisted of two T-shaped dining-rooms, long, narrow and low, one of which drew its light from the Place de la Sorbonne, the other from the Rue Neuve-de-Richelieu.'[22] Dinner cost eighteen sous, with a small carafe of wine or a bottle of beer, and twenty-two sous with a bottle of wine. Lucien de Rubempré had only a few steps to take to get there from the Hôtel de Cluny. He 'dropped into Flicoteaux's at about four-thirty, having observed that it paid to be among the first arrivals, for then the food was more varied and the customer could still obtain his favourite dishes'. It was there that he met the journalist Étienne Lousteau, 'a thin and pale young man, probably as poor as himself, whose handsome face, already withered, showed that vanished hopes had fatigued his brow and left furrows in his soul where the seeds sown had failed to germinate'.[23] It was also there that Lucien met another important figure, d'Arthez, who facilitated his admission to the Cénacle, that nursery of great men on Rue des Quatre-Vents. Thus, Flicoteaux served as a springboard for Lucien de Rubempré to enter the world of journalism, the book trade, the theatre and pretty girls, in which the rest of *Lost Illusions* takes place.

From Rastignac to Lucien de Rubempré, Lousteau to d'Arthez, Raphaël de Valentin to Bianchon, many of the characters in *The Human Comedy* at one time or another frequented the northern slope of Montagne Sainte-Geneviève, or the Latin Quarter. To the south, on the other hand, the slope that descends from the Panthéon to the Gobelins and the valley of the Bièvre, before climbing back up towards the Barrière d'Italie – that is, along the Faubourg Saint-Marceau – we meet only one character, but he is not just anyone.

> 'Monsieur,' said Derville, 'to whom have I the honour of speaking?'
> 'To Colonel Chabert.'
> 'Which one?'
> 'He who was killed at Eylau,' replied the old man.[24]

Derville, always helpful in the face of distress, after listening at length to the colonel's story – his wife has remarried, robbed him, and does not want to hear of him – lends him some money and goes to see where he lives:

> Colonel Chabert . . . was lodging in the Faubourg Saint-Marceau, Rue du Petit-Banquier, with an old quartermaster of the Imperial Guard now a cowkeeper, named Vergniaud. Having reached the spot, Derville was obliged to go on foot in search of his client, for his coachman declined to drive along an unpaved street, where the ruts were rather too deep for cab wheels. Looking about him on all sides, the lawyer at last discovered at the end of the street nearest the boulevard, between two walls built out of bones and mud, two shabby stone gateposts, much knocked about by carts, in spite of two wooded stumps that served as blocks. These posts supported a cross beam topped by a coping of tiles, and on the beam, in red letters, were the words: 'Vergniaud, dairyman'.[25]

Balzac describes Chabert's lodgings at length:

> The large pot-bellied tin cans in which the milk is carried, and the little pots for cream, were flung pell-mell at the dairy door, with their linen-covered stoppers. The rags that were used to clean them fluttered in the sunshine, riddled with holes, hanging to strings fastened to poles . . . A goat was munching the shoots of a

starved and dusty vine that clung to the cracked yellow wall of the house. A cat, squatting on the cream jars, was licking them over. The fowls, scared by Derville's approach, scuttered away screaming, and the watchdog barked. 'And the man who decided the victory at Eylau is to be found here!' said Derville to himself, as his eyes took in at a glance the general effect of the squalid scene.[26]

A muddy and miserable suburb, of course, but it is from its high point that the fourth chapter of *A Woman of Thirty* unfolds a grand vision, a sunny Paris – a fairyland, as Balzac himself writes:

Between the Barrière d'Italie and the Barrière de la Santé, along the boulevard which leads to the Jardin des Plantes, you have a view of Paris fit to send an artist or tourist, the most blasé in matters of landscape, into ecstasies. Reach the slightly higher ground where the line of boulevard, shaded by tall, thick-spreading trees, curves with the grace of some green and silent forest avenue, and you see spread out at your feet a deep valley scattered with seemingly rural workshops, among green trees and the brown streams of the Bièvre or the Gobelins.

On the opposite slope, beneath some thousands of roofs packed close together like heads in a crowd, lurks the squalor of the Faubourg Saint-Marceau. The imposing cupola of the Panthéon, and the grim melancholy dome of the Val-du-Grâce, tower proudly up above a whole town, built like an amphitheatre; every tier being grotesquely represented by a crooked line of street, so that the two public monuments look like a huge pair of giants dwarfing into insignificance the poor little houses and the tallest poplars in the valley. To your left behold the Observatoire, the daylight, pouring athwart its windows and galleries, producing such fantastical strange effects that the building looks like a black spectral skeleton. Further yet in the distance rises the elegant lantern tower of the Invalides, soaring up between the bluish pile of the Luxembourg and the grey towers of Saint-Sulpice. From this standpoint the lines of the architecture are blended with green leaves and grey shadows, and change every moment with every aspect of the heavens, every alteration of light or colour in the sky. Afar, the air itself seems full of buildings; near, wind the serpentine curves of waving trees and green footpaths.

Away to your right, through a great gap in this singular landscape, you see the Saint-Martin canal, a long pale stripe with its edging of reddish stone quays and fringes of lime avenue. The long rows of buildings beside it, in genuine Roman style, are the public granaries.

Beyond, again, on the very last plane of all, see the smoke-dimmed slopes of Belleville covered with houses and windmills, which blend their freaks of outline with the chance effects of cloud. And still, between that horizon, vague as some childish recollection, and the serried range of roofs in the valley, a whole city lies out of sight: a huge city, engulfed, as it were, in a vast hollow between the pinnacles of the Hôpital de la Pitié and the ridge line of the Cimetière de l'Est, between suffering on the one hand and death on the other; a city sending up a smothered roar like Ocean grumbling at the foot of a cliff, as if to let you know that 'I am here!'

When the sunlight pours like a flood over this strip of Paris, purifying and etherealizing the outlines, kindling answering lights here and there in the window panes, brightening the red tiles, flaming about the golden crosses, whitening walls and transforming the atmosphere into a gauzy veil, calling up rich contrasts of light and fantastic shadow; when the sky is blue and earth quivers in the heat and the bells are pealing, then you shall see one of the eloquent fairy scenes which stamp themselves for ever on the imagination, a scene that shall find as fanatical worshipers as the wondrous views of Naples and Byzantium or the isles of Florida. Nothing is wanting to complete the harmony, the murmur of the world of men and the idyllic quiet of solitude, the voices of a million human creatures and the voice of God. There lies a whole capital beneath the peaceful cypresses of Père-Lachaise.[27]

Adolphe Jean-Baptiste Bayot, *Père-Lachaise Cemetery*, lithograph, c. 1860
(Roger-Viollet)

The Faubourg Saint-Germain

The Faubourg Saint-Germain is the exact opposite of the
Faubourg Saint-Marceau, stretching along the plain, and as
noble as the other is proletarian. (Balzac does not often use this
word, which is nevertheless very much of his time; in 1832, when
the president of the Seine court of assizes asked Blanqui for
his profession, he replied: proletarian.) The Faubourg Saint-
Germain was created in the seventeenth century with the
subdivision of the vast domain of Queen Margot, Henry IV's
first wife: three streets parallel to the Seine, Rue de Bourbon
(now Rue de Lille), Rue de Verneuil and Rue de l'Université.
Initially, Balzac explains, this was an aristocratic district.
Then,

> the nobility, out of their element in the midst of shops, abandoned
> the Place Royale and the centre of Paris, and crossed the river to
> breathe at their ease in the Faubourg Saint-Germain . . . For

people accustomed to the splendours of life, is there indeed anything more unseemly than the tumult, the mud, the shouting, the bad smells and narrow streets of the populous quarters?[28]

At the time of *The Human Comedy*, the Faubourg Saint-Germain was a relatively old district, even though more recent streets, also parallel to the Seine – Rue de Grenelle, Rue Saint-Dominique, Rue de Varenne – extended it westwards. Balzac does not define its borders any more than he describes its architecture. The same man who devotes whole pages to the façade of the house of the Cat and Racket or the hovel in Rue du Tourniquet-Saint-Jean does not say a word about the Hôtel de Langeais, where the main part of the tragic love story between Antoinette de Navarreins, wife of the Duc de Langeais, and the Marquis de Montriveau, takes place.[29] We do not even know in which street it is located. The other mansions in the Faubourg are mentioned only in almost insignificant detail – a porch, a staircase, an address in passing. Of the Hôtel de Grandlieu – where Lucien de Rubempré, considering himself almost married to the daughter of the house, is left dumbstruck in the courtyard by the valet's dismissal ('Madame the duchesse has gone out') – we know only that it is 'one of the handsomest on Rue Saint-Dominique'. There are no details of the mansion on Rue de Bourbon where Calyste du Guénic settles with his young wife in *Béatrix*; nor do we know anything about Raphaël de Valentin's mansion on Rue de Varenne; nor that of the Comtesse Ferraud – wife of Colonel Chabert – on the same street (except that Derville is received in 'a pretty winter dining room'); or the one on Rue Plumet where the end of the strange episodic story of *A Woman of Thirty* takes place.[30]

This topographical and architectural vagueness has a reason: for Balzac, the Faubourg Saint-Germain was not a material territory but a state of mind:

> What is called in France the Faubourg Saint-Germain is neither a quarter of Paris nor a sect nor an institution, nor anything that can be precisely defined. There are great houses in the Place Royale, the Faubourg Saint-Honoré, and the Chaussée-d'Antin where people breathe the same air as in the Faubourg Saint-Germain. So the Faubourg is not entirely within the Faubourg. People born far from its influence can feel it and are attracted to this world, while certain others who are born there can be forever banished from it.[31]

Proust, who knew *The Human Comedy* as well as anyone, may have remembered this passage when he wrote of the Hôtel de Guermantes: 'The presence of the body of Jesus Christ in the host seemed to me no more obscure a mystery than this leading house in the Faubourg [Saint-Germain] being situated on the Right Bank of the river and so near that from my bedroom in the morning I could hear its carpets being beaten.'[32]

At the beginning of his great novella of the Faubourg Saint-Germain, *The Duchesse de Langeais*, Balzac exposes the errors and weaknesses that lost the aristocracy in 1830. (The action is set in the early 1820s, but Balzac, writing ten years later, often takes liberties with chronology.) 'Here and there in the Faubourg Saint-Germain, you encounter fine characters, but they are clear exceptions to the rule of general egoism that has caused the ruin of this world apart.' And further on:

> The Faubourg Saint-Germain played with batons, believing that they were power itself. It reversed the terms of the proposition that called it into existence. Instead of throwing away the insignia

that offended the people and quietly retaining its power, it allowed the bourgeoisie to seize authority, clung so fatally to its insignia, and constantly again forgot the laws that its numerical weakness decreed.

Or again: 'Instead of acting protector, like a great man, the Faubourg Saint-Germain was as greedy as an upstart. When the most intelligent nation in the world understood that the restored nobility had organized power and the budget to its own profit, it fell mortally ill. The nobility wanted to be an aristocracy when it could only be an oligarchy.'[33]

Nothing illustrates the has-been side of the Faubourg better than the family council held at the Hôtel de Langeais to quell the

The Duchesse de Langeais
(Bertall, Édition Furne)

scandal caused by the duchesse, who, as we saw, left her liveried carriage in front of the Marquis de Montriveau's mansion for a whole morning. In order to convince her to present the affair as a simple misunderstanding, 'four illustrious persons' met together, each 'belonging to that aristocratic sphere documented in the *Gotha Almanac*, which is devoted yearly to its revolutions and hereditary pretensions'. These were the Princesse de Blamont-Chauvry, aunt of the duchesse, who 'had such a high idea of her ruins that she would take her hair off in the evening, wear long gloves and still dye her cheeks with the classic Martin red'; the Vidame de Pamiers, 'another contemporary ruin', 'whose neck was always so tightly compressed by his collar that his cheeks hung slightly over his cravat and kept his head high – an attitude full of self-importance in some men but justified in his case by a Voltairean wit'; as well as the Duc de Navarreins and the Duc de Grandlieu:

> Both were fifty-five years of age, still healthy, corpulent and short, well fed, with slightly florid complexions, tired eyes, and already drooping lips. Without the exquisite tone of their language, without the affable polish of their manners, without their ease of manner that could suddenly become impertinence, a superficial observer might have taken them for bankers.[34]

This ironic and almost contemptuous tone can be explained by a kind of resentment, even a desire for revenge. When he wrote *The Duchesse de Langeais* in the early 1830s (it was published in 1834), Balzac was immersed in an unhappy love affair with a woman from the noble Faubourg, the Marquise de Castries, who manipulated him with the same coquetry that the duchesse displayed in holding Montriveau in the palm of her

hand. In 1836, in a letter to Louise, a mysterious correspondent
never identified, he wrote:

> It took five years of wounds for my tender nature to detach itself
> from an iron nature; a gracious woman, this quasi-duchess of
> whom I spoke, and who had come to me incognito so that, I give
> her this justice, she left the day I asked her: this liaison which,
> whatever one may say, know this well, has remained, by the will
> of this woman, in the most irreproachable conditions, has been one
> of the greatest sorrows of my life; the secret misfortunes of my
> present situation come from the fact that I sacrificed everything to
> her on the basis of a single desire of hers; she never guessed
> anything; the wounded man must be forgiven for fearing some
> injury. You speak to me of treasures, alas! do you know all those
> that I have dissipated on foolish hopes? I alone know what is terri-
> ble in *The Duchesse de Langeais*.[35]

For Stendhal, 'French high society is at present [1825] the
favourite haunt of boredom.'[36] In *Armance*, also a novel of the
Faubourg Saint-Germain, boredom is the background against
which the sad story of Octave's love affairs unfolds, and, in *Le
Rouge et le Noir*, there are 'those eyes [of Mathilde de la Mole] so
beautiful, in which the most profound boredom breathed'.
Nothing of the sort in Balzac, since with him, as Baudelaire says,

> all the characters are endowed with the same vital ardour as
> Balzac himself. All his fictions are as colourful as dreams. From
> the top of the aristocracy to the bottom of the plebs, all the actors
> in his *Comedy* are fiercer in life, more active and cunning in
> struggle, more patient in misfortune, more gullible in enjoyment,
> more angelic in devotion, than the comedy that the real world
> shows us. All souls are souls loaded with willpower up to their
> eye-teeth.[37]

So much so that, with Balzac, in the Faubourg Saint-Germain as elsewhere, there is no room for boredom.

Between the Montagne Sainte-Geneviève and the Faubourg Saint-Germain, the urban fabric was not fully connected in Balzac's time in the way that the VIth arrondissement is today: it was made up of small foci, each with its own population and atmosphere. Most of them were dirty and miserable – most, but not all. The Rue de Seine, stretching between the Institut Français and the Palais du Luxembourg, had a certain dignity; and around the Odéon theatre there were reading rooms and literary cafés such as the Café Voltaire, on the corner of Place and Rue de l'Odéon, or the Café Tabourey, on the corner of Rue Rotrou and Rue de Vaugirard. It was there that Alfred Delvau remembered seeing, 'as a small and obscure adolescent, the great and glorious M. de Balzac on the morning of the first performance of *Les Ressources de Quinola*'.[38]

But, in the central part of the Left Bank, the places where Balzac's characters evolve are the opposite of what they have become for us. In *The Black Sheep*, when Madame Bridau, ruined by the speculations of her son Philippe, is forced to leave her beautiful apartment on Quai Voltaire, she settles in

one of the most horrible corners of Paris . . . that portion of Rue Mazarine which runs from Rue Guénégard to the point at which it joins Rue de Seine, behind the Palais de l'Institut. The tall grey walls of the college and the library donated to the City of Paris by Cardinal Mazarin, and which were one day destined to house the Académie Française, cast icy shadows across this part of the street; sunshine is a rare sight, and an icy north wind blows along it. The poor ruined widow took up residence on the third floor of one of the houses in this damp, dark, cold corner.[39]

Not far from there, on Rue de Nevers, lived the charming old Schmucke, the friend of Cousin Pons, who gave piano lessons to the two daughters of the Comtesse de Granville. When the elder daughter, Marie, now Comtesse de Vandenesse, was desperate for money to pay the debts of the journalist she was in love with, she had the idea of getting Schmucke to sign bills of exchange on which she would guarantee payment. At eight o'clock in the morning, she arrived at Quai Conti:

> The carriage could not enter the narrow Rue de Nevers; but as Schmucke lived in a house at the corner of the quai she was not obliged to walk up its muddy pavement, but could jump from the step of her carriage to the broken step of the dismal old house, mended like porter's crockery, with iron rivets, and bulging out over the street in a way that was quite alarming to pedestrians.[40]

In the brief marvel that is *The Atheist's Mass*, the great Desplein, chief surgeon of the Hôtel-Dieu like his model Dupuytren, passes with his pupil Bianchon the Rue des Quatre-Vents, 'one of the worst streets in Paris'. He shows him the sixth floor of 'one of the houses looking like obelisks, of which the narrow door opens into a passage with a winding staircase at the end, with windows appropriately termed "borrowed lights" [*jours de souffrance*]'.[41] He tells him about his miserable youth, where he 'worked through a whole winter, seeing my head steam, and perceiving the atmosphere of my own moisture as we see that of horses on a frosty day'. It was in this same garret that the famous Cénacle – to which Lucien de Rubempré was introduced thanks to d'Arthez – later met nine friends, of whom 'each one of them, like d'Arthez, bore the stamp of genius upon his forehead'. They included Horace Bianchon; Joseph Bridau, 'one of the best painters of the young school'; Michel Chrestien, 'a republican with far-reaching ideas who dreamed of a European federation and in 1830 was to take a prominent place among the idealists of the Saint-Simonian movement' – he 'was to die as a common soldier in the massacre of the Cloister of Saint-Merri'.[42] Continuing along Rue des Quatre-Vents, you reach Saint-Sulpice, a deserted district, ideal for those in hiding. It was there, in Rue Cassette, that Abbé Carlos Herrera (alias Vautrin) lived with his Lucien, in *A Harlot High and Low*. He 'lived, moreover, very obscurely, as traditionally did priests employed on secret missions. He fulfilled his religious duties at Saint-Sulpice, and only went out on business, always in the evening and by carriage.' A stone's throw away, on Rue Honoré-Chevalier, we find Corentin, the former evil genius of Fouché, head of Louis XVIII's secret police, who plays a major role in the disaster that befalls Lucien at the end of the book.

As you move away from the centre, the misery is doubled by the thickness of the mud – it was not by chance that the large maternity hospital south of the Luxembourg was called La Bourbe.[43] When Lucien de Rubempré tries to read his 'Marguerites' to Lousteau, a journalist whose 'benevolence he hoped to parade in order to find a publisher or to get into the newspaper', they go 'to sit under the trees in that part of Luxembourg which, from the large Allée de l'Observatoire, leads to Rue de l'Ouest. This street was then a long quagmire, lined with planks and marshes where the only houses were towards Rue de Vaugirard.'[44] Nearby, Godefroid, who had become 'the Initiate' and was roaming Paris to spread the word, arrives in 'Rue Notre-Dame-des-Champs at the point where it joins Rue de l'Ouest, neither of which was paved at the time'. He is surprised 'to find great mud-holes in that fine open quarter. Persons walked on planks laid down beside the houses and along the marshy gardens, or on narrow paths flanked on each side by stagnant water which sometimes turned them into rivulets.'[45]

When you leave these deprived areas and return to the centre, approaching Rue des Marais-Saint-Germain where Balzac had his print shop, you enter the realm of books (this was still true twenty years ago, before publishing migrated to smoked glass and metal buildings near the Périphérique).[46] All the great and not so great publishers of the Romantic period lived and worked in the same streets: Urbain Canel, the publisher of *Armance*, who brought out Balzac's first signed novel (*The Chouans*) in 1829, lived on Place Saint-André-des-Arts; Mame, who published *A Country Doctor* after many ups and downs, was on Rue Guénégaud; Werdet, the publisher of *Old Man Goriot*, *The Firm of Nucingen*, and *The Lily of the Valley*, who went bankrupt for not having resisted Balzac's demands for money, was on Rue de Seine, as was Hetzel, the driving force behind the definitive edition of *The Human Comedy*. Gosselin, the greatest Romantic publisher, whose authors included Victor Hugo, Alphonse de Lamartine, and George Sand, and who published *The Wild Ass's Skin*, was at 9 Rue Saint-Germain-des-Prés. Souverain was at 5 Rue des Beaux-Arts, and Charpentier, inventor of cheap mass printings, was at no. 6 on the same street.[47]

Along the Seine, on Quais Conti, Malaquais and Voltaire, books were still to be found, but on stalls or from wholesalers such as Vidal and Porchon, to whom Lucien de Rubempré proposed his novel *The Archer of Charles the Ninth* – soon realizing that 'books, like cotton nightcaps, were to be regarded as articles of merchandise to be sold dear and bought cheap'. There were also print and antique dealers, like the one that Raphaël enters, deciding to throw himself into the water after losing his last Louis d'or at the Palais-Royal – he would emerge with the magic ass's skin.

In *The Human Comedy*, the Seine is not the great river that structures the city but rather an invitation to suicide for young people discouraged by life. The only exception is at the beginning of *The Brotherhood of Consolation*, where Godefroid, who is not yet the initiate and is looking for a meaning to his life, is

> leaning against the parapet of this quay from which one can see both the Seine upstream from the Jardin des Plantes as far as Notre-Dame, and downstream the vast prospect of the river as far as the Louvre. No view is comparable in the capital of ideas . . . The cupola of Sainte-Geneviève towers above the Latin Quarter. Behind us rises the noble apsis of the cathedral. The Hôtel de Ville tells of revolutions; the Hôtel-Dieu of the miseries of Paris . . . This spot, the heart of ancient Paris, is the loneliest and most melancholy of regions. The waters of the Seine break there noisily, the cathedral casts its shadows at the setting of the sun. We can easily believe that serious thoughts must have filled the mind of a man afflicted with a moral malady.[48]

The Right Bank

Crossing the Seine, one entered a more populated and more prosperous Paris, full of great restaurants, luxury tailors and places of pleasure. There were also wretched places, but they were like isolated pockets, except for the working-class suburbs in the east, which Balzac rarely mentions. It is in this city of merchants, artists, parvenus, bankers, and a few aristocrats that many episodes of *The Human Comedy* take place.

Balzac distinguishes two strata of Paris, the old and the new. The former is contained within the arc of the Grands Boulevards, the 'enchanted promenade' between Madeleine and Bastille. Still largely medieval in its architecture and the jumble of its streets, it had hardly changed since the end of the Ancien Régime. But under the July Monarchy, 'in fifteen years, a second Paris was built between the hills of Montmartre and the line of the Midi', that is, between the boulevards and the Wall of the Farmers-General that bounded the city.[49] Balzac saw this new Paris develop before his eyes. The emergence of entire districts, financial speculation, the constructions of the *nouveaux riches* – this is the background noise of *The Human Comedy*, an incomparable picture of the formation of a city. In his inaugural lecture at the Collège de France, Louis Chevalier, a demographer and historian of Paris, explained to an audience who were perhaps rather surprised, that Balzac's work said more than statistics and archival documents. And, in fact, to understand the financial manipulations that surrounded the construction of the Madeleine district, *César Birotteau* is essential reading. Similarly, *Béatrix* describes the difficult beginnings of the Europe quarter, 'in those solitudes of sculpted rubble that furnish the quarter's streets named after Amsterdam, Milan, Stockholm, London, and Moscow, architectural steppes where the wind blows innumerable signs that accuse the emptiness of the district by these words: Apartments to rent!'[50]

Old Paris: From the Concorde to the Bastille

This was bounded on the west by the stone bridge spanning the moat that separated the Tuileries Garden from Place Louis XVI (Place de la Concorde after 1830). The characters of *The Human Comedy* whom we meet here are not the same as those in the Luxembourg, a shady garden conducive to solitary reverie and discussion among friends. The Tuileries was, on the contrary, a sunny garden where one went to admire and be admired. It was here, 'on one of those beautiful spring mornings, when the leaves, though unfolded, are not yet green, when the sun is beginning to set the roofs ablaze and the sky is blue', that de Marsay meets 'the girl with the golden eyes'. When Staub, the great rival tailor of Buisson, brings Lucien de Rubempré a new suit, he tells him: 'A young man dressed like that can go for a walk in the Tuileries, he will marry a rich Englishwoman within a fortnight.'[51]

The gardens were closed off to the east by the Château des Tuileries. At the beginning of *A Woman of Thirty*, the young Julie d'Aiglemont attends with her father the review of the Imperial Guard in the courtyard of the château before the army left for Russia. She was astonished to see 'an immense crowd penned up in a narrow space, shut in between the grey walls of the palace and the limits marked out by chains round the great sanded squares in the midst of the courtyard of the Tuileries'. In a long and magnificent description of the movement of the troops, Balzac lets us glimpse the Napoleonic spirit that he would keep throughout his life: 'The existence of the French Empire was at stake – to be, or not to be. The whole citizen population seemed to be as much inspired with this thought as that other armed population standing in serried and silent ranks in the enclosed space, with the Eagles and the spirit of Napoleon hovering above them.'[52]

A few steps away, huddled against the Louvre, the small Carrousel district was being demolished in Balzac's time, though parts of it were still intact in the 1840s. Baudelaire evokes it in 'The Swan': 'I see only in my mind this whole field of shacks, / These piles of rough-hewn capitals and shafts, / The grasses, the large blocks greened by the water of the puddles, / And, shining in the windows, the confused bric-a-brac.' Balzac gives a very dark vision of this neighbourhood where Cousin Bette lived:

> Rue du Doyenné and the blind alley of the same name are the only passages that penetrate this sombre and deserted block, inhabited presumably by ghosts, for one never catches sight of anyone here. The footway, standing much lower than the pavement of Rue du Musée, comes out on a level with Rue Froid-manteau. These houses, submerged and darkened by the raising of the square, also lie wrapped in the perpetual shadow cast by the high galleries of the Louvre, blackened on this side by the north wind. The gloom, the silence, the glacial air, the hollow sunken ground level, combine to make these houses seem so many crypts. If, passing in a cab through this dead area, one happens to glance down the Impasse du Doyenné, a chill strikes one's heart, one wonders who can possibly live here and what may happen here at night, at the hour when the alley becomes a place of cut-throats, when the vices of Paris, shrouded in night's mantle, move as they will.[53]

The Carrousel quarter is not the only poor and sad place in that brilliant region of old Paris between the Louvre, the

Palais-Royal and Place Vendôme. At the beginning of *A Harlot High and Low*, the beautiful Ésther lives on Rue de Langlade, a small street between Rue Traversière and Rue Sainte-Anne:

> Rue de Langlade, like the adjacent streets, runs between the Palais-Royal and Rue de Rivoli. This part of one of the smartest districts of Paris will long preserve the contamination it received from those hillocks that were the middens of old Paris, topped with windmills. These narrow streets, dark and muddy, where trades are carried on which do not care about external appearance, take on at night a mysterious physiognomy . . . Passers-by walk quickly and are uncommon. The shops are shut, those still open have an unsavoury character: a dirty wine shop without lights, a linen-draper's selling eau de Cologne. An unwholesome chill folds its damp mantle about your shoulders.[54]

It is understandable that Esther was happy to move to Rue Taitbout with her Lucien.

Not far from there, at the beginning of *Ferragus*, Baron de Maulincourt recognizes by chance one evening in the street 'a chaste and delightful person, with whom he was secretly and passionately in love – a love without hope; she was married'. The scene takes place in Rue Pagevin, 'in the days when that street had no wall which did not echo some infamous word, and was, in the direction of Rue Soly, the narrowest and most impassable street in Paris'. The baron was stunned: 'his knowledge did not permit him to be ignorant of all there was of possible infamy in an elegant, rich, young, and beautiful woman walking there, alone, with a furtively criminal step'.[55] This is the beginning of a fatal misunderstanding from which both characters end up dead.

These miserable pockets rub shoulders with the most elegant parts of the city, centred on the Palais-Royal, the most famous place in the western world at the time of Balzac's youth. Before the cutting of Avenue de l'Opéra and the construction of the Guichets du Louvre, it was wide open to the city: to reach the Tuileries from the Palais-Royal, Henri de Marsay only had to cross Rue Saint-Honoré and Rue de Rivoli. Since the Directory period, the pleasures of the day had been concentrated there, so much so that the English, Prussian, Russian, and Austrian officers who entered Paris in 1815 had only one idea in mind, to dine and gamble at the Palais-Royal.

The gaming houses had no name but a number, that of the arcade where they were located.[56] At the beginning of *The Wild Ass's Skin*, Raphaël climbs the stairs to the gambling den known as No. 36. The old players

> at their first glance . . . were able to read some horrible mystery in the newcomer's face. His youthful features were stamped with a clouded grace and the look in his eyes bore witness to efforts betrayed and to a thousand hopes deceived . . . But the young man walked straight up to the table, remained standing, and blindly threw on to the cloth a gold coin he had been holding. It rolled on to black . . . 'Red wins,' the dealer proclaimed.[57]

Raphaël has lost his last napoleon; all that remains for him is to throw himself into the Seine. In *Old Man Goriot*, Rastignac plays the contents of the purse entrusted to him by his mistress, Delphine de Nucingen, on number 9. He 'staked the whole of his money on the number 21 (his own age). There was a cry of surprise; before he knew what he had done, he had won. "Take your money off, sir," said the old gentleman; "you don't often win twice running by that system."'

Taking the rake the old man was holding out to him, Eugène swept the three thousand six hundred francs towards him and, still not knowing how the game worked, staked them on the red. The gallery watched him enviously, seeing him play again. The wheel turned, he won once more and the croupier pushed another three thousand six hundred francs his way.

'You now have seven thousand two hundred francs,' murmured the old man in his ear. 'If I were you I'd leave; the red has come up eight times. If you're feeling charitable, you'll acknowledge this sound advice by relieving the poverty of one of Napoleon's old prefects, who is down to his last penny.'

In a daze, Rastignac let the white-haired man take ten louis, then went back down the stairs with his seven thousand francs, still knowing nothing at all about the game but staggered by his good luck.[58]

Balzac does not mention the most famous of the gambling houses in the Palais-Royal, No. 113 – eight tables of trente et quarante, six of roulette – where it is said that Blücher lost so much money that, when he left Paris, all his lands were pledged. Was Balzac himself a gambler? Perhaps, if we believe the recollections of Werdet, one of his editors. He tells us that, one evening, Balzac borrowed twenty francs from him and sent Jules Sandeau to play them at No. 113, explaining his infallible system. The twenty francs were lost, and another forty that Balzac borrowed from 'his heraldic engraver, under the arcades, next to the Café de Foy . . . "We must resign ourselves," Honoré said philosophically, "Fortune is against us!"'[59]

Gambling brings with it another activity, that of paid love affairs. In the evening, lovely ladies descend from the upper floors and crowd the arcades and gaming rooms – some even lend money to the players. Their pretty clothes contribute to the colour and charm of the Palais-Royal.

Another attraction of the place is the dining table. We remember that little Félix de Vandenesse, punished by his mother, was deprived of the dinner planned at the Frères Provençaux, but the most famous restaurant, one of the two great ones in *The Human Comedy* (the other being the Rocher de Cancale, Rue Montorgueil), is Véry. Balzac often dined there with friends. 'One has one's own table, one dines at one's leisure, without distraction, in the open air, the cooking is fine and one can say like Titus, after sitting six hours at table: "I have used my day well." '[60] The bill was accordingly high. Lucien de Rubempré,

> reluctant to linger among the ruins of his self-esteem . . . went into Véry's restaurant and, to initiate himself in the pleasures of Paris, ordered such a dinner as might console him in his despondency. A bottle of claret, oysters from Ostend, fish, a partridge, a macaroni dish and fruit were the *ne plus ultra* of his desires . . . He was torn from his dreams by the bill for the meal which relieved him of the fifty francs which he thought would carry him a long way in Paris. His dinner had cost him as much as a month's existence in Angoulême.[61]

Among the many cafés housed under the arcades, the most famous was the Café de Foy, in the Galerie de Montpensier, the only one authorized to sell ice cream and drinks in the garden. Balzac had a predilection for the Café des Mille Colonnes whose owner, *la belle limonadière*, was considered one of the prettiest women in Paris. When César Birotteau met Constance, the first lady of the Petit Matelot, in a novelty shop on Quai d'Anjou at the corner of Pont Marie, Balzac wrote that 'she was at that time cited for her beauty, as was the case in later days with *la belle limonadière* of the Café des Mille Colonnes, and several other poor creatures who flattened more noses, young and old, against the window-panes of milliners, confectioners, and linen-drapers, than there are stones in the streets of Paris'.[62] In the Beaujolais gallery was the Café Lemblin, a haunt of officers on half-pay where the waiters had swords at the disposal of customers who wished to duel. Philippe Brideau – the favourite son of his mother, whom his antics would cause to move, as we have seen, to the dreadful Rue Mazarine – when he went from being a lieutenant-colonel with a salary of nine thousand francs to a half-pay at three hundred francs, became 'one of the Bonapartists most frequently found at the Café Lemblin, a real constitutionalist backwater'.[63]

In Balzac's time, the most animated corner of the Palais-Royal was what were known as the Galeries de Bois, stretching from one wing to the other on the site of the present colonnade. They were

shanties, or more exactly wood huts made of planks, poorly roofed, small, dimly lit on the court and garden side by indirect lights of suffrance which passed for windows, but which in fact were more like the dirtiest kind of aperture found in the taverns beyond the city gates. A triple range of shops formed two galleries about twelve feet high. Shops sited in the centre looked out on to the two galleries, from which they borrowed their pestilential atmosphere and whose roofing allowed only a little light to filter through invariably dirty window-panes . . . This agglomeration reminiscent of a gypsy camp or the booths on a fairground – the sort of temporary construction which Paris heaps about the monuments it fails to build – this contorted physiognomy was wonderfully in keeping with the teeming variety of trades carried on beneath these brazenly indecent hutments, noisy with babble and hectic with gaiety, and where an enormous amount of business has been transacted between the two Revolutions of 1789 and 1830 . . . It was the home ground of publishers, poets, pedlars of prose,

politicians, milliners and, lastly the prostitutes who roamed about
it in the evenings.[64]

The booksellers in question specialised in novelties: light and
amusing books. It was there that Dauriat operated, to whom
Lucien de Rubempré finally sold his collection of poems, *Les
Marguerites*, after many ups and downs. However, there was a
great bookseller and publisher, Levavasseur, who published
Canel's *Physiologie du mariage* in 1829. The Galeries de Bois
were destroyed in 1828 and replaced by a covered gallery, built
by Fontaine, of which only the columns remain today.

The date on which the decline of the Palais-Royal began is
as well-known as those of the great fire of London or the Lisbon
earthquake: on 31 December 1836, gambling was banned in
Paris. With the closure of its gambling dens, the Palais-Royal
lost most of its charm, and the centre of gravity for pleasures
shifted a few hundred metres to the north, to the 'enchanted
promenade' of the boulevards. Balzac does not mention the
event directly, but the Palais-Royal disappears from those
novels of *The Human Comedy* which are set after the mid-
1830s. The Paris Balzac describes evolves according to the
dates when the novels are set – not, of course, when they were
written. But as Balzac grows older, these dates often come
closer together: several late masterpieces are set very close to
the time of writing. Thus *Cousin Bette*, completed in the autumn
of 1846, takes place between 1838 and 1845, and *Cousin Pons*,
completed in 1847, is dated in the very first line: 'About three
o'clock in the afternoon, one day in October 1844, an old man
of some sixty years . . .'

One of Balzac's tricks is to have aged the characters throughout *The Human Comedy* in novels that are not written in

chronological order. The brilliant and giddy Diane de Maufrigneuse becomes the wise Princesse de Cadignan; Rastignac,
whom we knew as a young student at the Vauquer boarding-
house in *Old Man Goriot*, ends up as a count, peer of the realm
and minister of justice in *The Deputy for Arcis*; as for the illustrious de Marsay, he dies: 'The count and countess [de Vandenesse]
went to Lady Dudley's grand ball, where, by the bye, de Marsay
appeared in society for the last time. He died about two months
later, leaving the reputation of a great statesman, because, as
Blondet remarked, his influence was beyond comprehension.'[65]
The restoration of the passage of time strengthens the unity of
the work and makes the architecture of the Balzacian cathedral
more concrete.

   If *The Duchesse de Langeais* is the great novel of the Faubourg
Saint-Germain and *Cousin Pons* that of the Marais, it is in the
adventures of César Birotteau that the 'commercial' district is
depicted, stretching along Rue Saint-Honoré from Rue Royale
to Rue de Richelieu. 'Birotteau is a masterpiece,' Balzac's friend
Delphine de Girardin wrote to him, and one can understand her
enthusiasm for a book so rich that it can be read on several levels.
First of all, it is the portrait of a man. Birotteau is a perfumer at
the Reine des Roses, Rue Saint-Honoré, 'near Place Vendôme'.
He made his fortune with his 'Paste of Sultans' and 'Carminative
Balm', and was preparing to launch 'Cephalic Oil', advised by
a great scientist of the time, the chemist Vauquelin. He is remarkable for his inventiveness and broad-mindedness, which allows
him to marry his daughter Césarine to his poor, lame clerk,
Anselme Popinot, whose future he will ensure. But he has ridic-
ulous sides – his vanity, his way of recalling his deeds ('On
Vendémaire I was wounded at Saint-Roch').[66] Some of his traits

evoke the follies of Balzac himself: he spends a fortune enlarging and decorating his apartment in preparation for a ball he is to give to celebrate his Légion d'honneur – Chevet would provide the silver, the dinner, the wine, the waiters; he engages in dubious speculation, planning to buy 'in the vicinity of the Madeleine, land which we shall get for a quarter of the value it is bound to reach in three years'.[67]

In the second part, 'César Grappling with Misfortune', Balzac undoubtedly draws on his own experience. He describes the perverse mechanism organized by Du Tillet to ruin his former boss and recover his spoils (Du Tillet is the worst scoundrel in *The Human Comedy*, starting out by stealing three thousand francs from the till of his employer Birotteau, and ending up a great banker and member of parliament). This is followed by details of what a bankruptcy was like under the Restoration, the roles of the Juge-Commissaire, the Agent des Créanciers, the Syndics – long passages in which Balzac undoubtedly remembers what he endured at the time of the disaster of his print shop.

César Birotteau also sheds light on the shop-keeping class of this neighbourhood:

> The bourgeoisie of Rue Saint-Denis displayed itself majestically [at the famous ball] in the plenitude of its native powers of jocose silliness. It was a fair spectrum of that middle class which dresses its children like lancers or national guards, buys the *Victoires et Conquêtes*, the *Soldat-laboureur*, admires the *Convoi du Pauvre*, delights in mounting guard, goes on Sunday to its own country-house, is anxious to acquire the distinguished air, and dreams of municipal honours – that middle class which is jealous of all and every one, and yet is good, obliging, devoted, feeling, compassionate, ready to subscribe for the children of General Foy, or for the

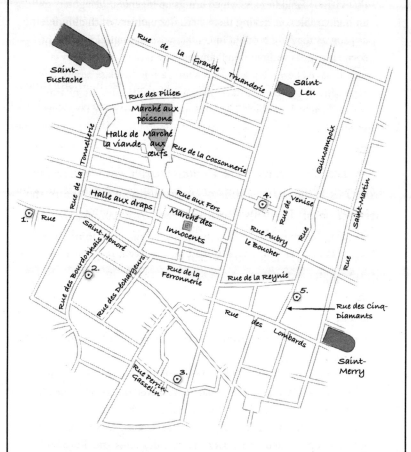

Les Halles in the time of César Birotteau

1. Rue de la Monnaie, Café David
2. Rue des Bourdonnais, the home of Uncle Pillerault
3. Rue Perrin-Gasselin, Mother Madou's shop
4. Cour Batave, the home of Molineux
5. Rue des Cinq-Diamants, Popinot's ironmonger's shop

Greeks, whose piracies it knows nothing about, or the Champ-
d'Asile until it no longer existed; duped through its virtues and
scouted for its defects by a social class that is not worthy of it, for
it has a heart precisely because it is ignorant of social conventions –
that virtuous middle class which brings up ingenuous daughters to
an honourable toil, giving them sterling qualities which diminish
as soon as they are brought in contact with the superior world of
social life; girls without mind, among whom the worthy Chrysale
would have chosen his wife – in short, a middle class admirably
represented by the Matifats, druggists in Rue des Lombards,
whose firm had supplied 'The Queen of Roses' for more than sixty
years.[68]

In Balzac's time, the Saint-Honoré quarter was not as distinct
from Les Halles as it is today – or rather as it was before the
destruction of the 1970s. Birotteau had many contacts beyond
Rue Saint-Jacques-de-la-Boucherie (now the course of Rue du
Louvre, the current border). When he needed hazelnuts to make
his 'Cephalic Oil', he went to find

a certain Madame Angélique Madou, living on Rue Perrin-
Gasselin, the sole establishment which kept the true filbert of
Provence, and the veritable white hazelnut of the Alps. Rue
Perrin-Gasselin is one of the narrow thoroughfares in a square
labyrinth enclosed by the Quai, Rue Saint-Denis, Rue de la
Ferronnerie and Rue de la Monnaie; it is, as it were, one of the
entrails of the city. There swarm an infinite number of heterogeneous and mixed articles of merchandise, evil-smelling and
jaunty, herrings and muslin, silks and honey, butter and gauze, and
above all a number of petty trades, of which Paris knows as little
as a man knows of what is going on in his pancreas, and which, at
the present moment, had a blood-sucker named Bidault, other-
wise called Gigonnet, a money-lender, who lived on Rue Grénetat.
In this quarter old stables were filled with oil-casks, and the

carriage-houses were packed with bales of cotton. Here were stored in bulk the articles that were sold at retail in the markets.[69]

Thanks to Birotteau, little Popinot settled in Rue des Cinq-Diamants,

> a narrow little street where loaded wagons can scarcely pass each other, [which] runs from Rue des Lombards at one end to Rue Aubry-le-Boucher at the other, entering the latter opposite to Rue Quincampoix, that famous thoroughfare of old Paris where French history has so often been enacted. In spite of this disadvantage, the congregation of druggists in that neighbourhood made Popinot's choice of the little street a good one.[70]

Molineux, the landlord from whom Birotteau bought his neighbour's flat for the famous ball, lived in the Cour Batave, between Rue de Venise and Rue Saint-Denis:

> This cloistral structure, with arcades and interior galleries built of free-stone, with a fountain at one end – a parched fountain, that opens its lion's mouth less to give water than to ask for it from the passers-by – was doubtless invented to endow the Saint-Denis quarter with a species of Palais-Royal . . . there are various industrial cloaca, very few Batavians, but a great many grocers.[71]

Pillerault, the uncle who watched over Madame Birotteau, and 'belonged to this section of working people raised by the revolution to the bourgeoisie', lived on Rue des Bourdonnais and frequented the Café David, on the corner of Rue de la Monnaie and Rue Saint-Honoré, 'a meeting-place for old, retired merchants or wholesale dealers still in the game: Camusots, Lebas, Pilleraults, Popinots, a few landowners like Little Father Molineux'.[72] It is by such details, fragments of notes and the

magic of names, that Balzac makes us feel the rumble of the
Halles quarter (he often says '*la halle*') – of which Nerval, rather
later, would give a vision that is rather close despite the dif-
ference in style: 'Under the columns of the potato market,
early-rising or tardive women peeled their produce by the light
of lanterns. There were pretty ones who worked under the eye
of their mothers, singing old songs.'[73]

The Marais of Cousin Pons was a smaller quarter than today's,
when estate agents have pushed its boundaries beyond anything
reasonable: bounded by Rue des Francs-Bourgeois, Rue Vieille-
du-Temple and Boulevard Beaumarchais, this was a quiet
neighbourhood quarter, a little withdrawn from the city – as it
still was even in the 1950s. Pons lived with his friend Schmucke
in a calm house on Rue de Normandie, 'one of those streets in
which you might feel you were in a provincial town. Grass
thrives there, a passer-by is a rare occurrence, and everybody
knows everybody else.'[74] A failed composer, he ran an orchestra
that accompanied ballets and fantasies in a theatre created by
Gaudissart, the former commercial traveller who had assured
the success of Birroteau's 'Cephalic Oil'. His friend Schmucke,
an excellent musician, saw to the instrumentation of Pons's
scores.

The isolation of the Marais can be judged by the list of characters in *Cousin Pons*: there are none of the usual protagonists of
The Human Comedy, but rather caretakers, a second-hand dealer,
a fortune teller, and people of little means. When Pons is ill, it is
not Bianchon who comes to his bedside but a doctor named Pou-
lain, 'who, thanks to the esteem of the concierges in his district,
has managed to gain a small clientele that is barely sufficient for
his needs'. There is no mention in *The Human Comedy* of the

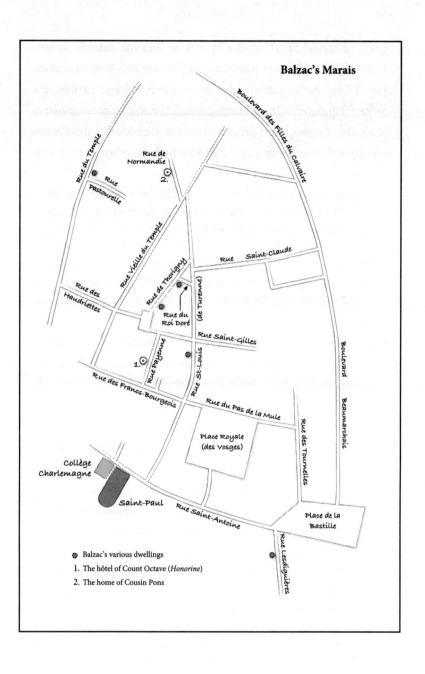

Balzac's Marais

Rue du Temple

Rue de Normandie

2.

Rue Pastourelle

Boulevard des Filles du Calvaire

Rue Vieille du Temple

Rue Saint-Claude

Rue de Thorigny

Rue des Haudriettes

(de Turenne)

Rue du Roi Doré

Rue Saint-Gilles

Rue Saint-Louis

Rue Payenne

1.

Rue des Francs-Bourgeois

Rue du Pas de la Mule

Boulevard Beaumarchais

Place Royale (des Vosges)

Rue des Tournelles

Collège Charlemagne

Saint-Paul

Rue Saint-Antoine

Place de la Bastille

Rue Lesdiguières

● Balzac's various dwellings
1. The hôtel of Count Octave (*Honorine*)
2. The home of Cousin Pons

great historical hôtels of the Marais, except in *Honorine*, where
Count Octave lives on Rue Payenne, 'in a mansion as vast as the
Hôtel Carnavalet, situated between courtyard and garden, but
quite dilapidated'. The avocat-général Granville, protagonist of
A Double Family, lives on the corner of Rue Vieille-du-Temple
and Rue Neuve-Saint-François (now Debelleyme):

> The lawyer wished to live in the Chaussée-d'Antin, where
> everything is fresh and bright, where the fashions may be seen
> while still new, where a well-dressed crowd throngs the boule-
> vards, and where the distance is less to the theatres or places of
> amusement; but he was obliged to give way to the coaxing ways
> of a young wife, who asked this as a first favour; so, to please her,
> he buried himself in the Marais.[75]

He *buried* himself: the word sums up the atmosphere of the Marais
in Balzac's time. Even restaurants that were elegant when he was
a young student had become very much out of fashion: 'The
famous Cadran Bleu doesn't have a window or a floor that is
level.' As for the Café Turc, which in *Bureaucracy* (1835) was still
'the meeting place for the elegant men and women of the Marais,
the Faubourg Saint-Antoine and the surrounding areas', it was
now 'to fashion what the ruins of Thebes are to civilization'.[76]

Balzac was cruel to the Marais where he had lived for so long,
but he was not alone. For Louis-Sébastien Mercier,

> the Marais is to the brilliant district of the Palais-Royal what
> Vienna is to London. Here reigns, not misery, but a complete heap
> of all damaged people: ruined men take refuge there. You see
> grumbling and gloomy old men, enemies of all new ideas; while
> impetuous advisers, unable to read, lambast authors whose names
> reach them: philosophers are called *men for burning*.[77]

Even in the middle of the twentieth century, the Marais was still a dark and dirty district, cut off from the general movement of the city. Its transformation into the present disaster zone began only with the 'renovation' of the 1960s.

Between the moats of the Tuileries and the Bastille, Old Paris did not remain static during Balzac's Parisian years. The writer was attentive to the destruction of the medieval Halles and the surrounding Carrousel quarter. He observed the work around the Hôtel de Ville, which was being extended towards the Seine. In the labyrinth of alleys behind that building – Rue du Tourniquet-Saint-Jean, Rue du Martroi, Rue de la Tixerandrie, where episodes of *A Double Family* and *A Harlot High and Low* are set – demolition began in the early 1830s. He also saw the development of the Seine embankments, converted from mere riverbanks into quays, and noticed in passing one of the most important projects launched by the prefect Rambuteau: the levelling of the rollercoaster that was the boulevards between Porte Saint-Denis and Château d'Eau. At the beginning of *History of a Crime*, Victor Hugo walks along the boulevard on the first day of Louis Bonaparte's coup d'état: 'The recent levelling of the road had converted Boulevard de la Porte-Saint-Martin into a deep cutting, commanded by two embankments. On the summits of these embankments were the footways. The carriages drove along the cutting, the foot passengers walked along the footways.'[78]

The boulevards are not only a topographical landmark, the border between old and new Paris, they are 'this asphalt sheet on which, from one o'clock to two, it is difficult not to see some of the characters for whom Fame blows one or other of her trumpets', as the painter Léon de Lora and the clever Bixiou explain

to a provincial cousin in *The Unconscious Comedians*. This asphalt
sheet is continuous: omnibuses run from the Madeleine to the
Bastille without encountering either a square or a major inter-
section. If the route is divided, it is by differences in population,
shops and theatres, not by major gaps such as Place de l'Opéra,
the Richelieu-Drouot crossroads or Place de la République.

Balzac devoted a monograph to this 'enchanted promenade', *Histoire et physiologie des boulevards de Paris*, published
in *Le Diable à Paris* in 1845.[79] His itinerary begins at the
Madeleine, 'a great and beautiful thing, whatever one may say,
but spoiled by the infamous café sculptures that disgrace the
side friezes'. From there to Rue Caumartin, 'one passes, but
does not linger. This part is without animation, although the
passer-by is generally well dressed, elegant and rich.' This is
because it is spoiled by a street which doubles it downwards,
built in the old ditch of the enclosure: 'As long as Rue Basse-
du-Rempart, the last of the low streets, exists, this boulevard
will have neither gaiety, nor character, nor strollers, nor sales
as a result.'

After Rue de la Paix, we reach 'the heart of present-day Paris,
which pulsates between Rue de la Chaussée-d'Antin and Rue du
Faubourg-Montmartre. There begin those strange and marvellous buildings which are all a fantastic tale or a few pages from
The Thousand and One Nights': the Pavillon de Hanovre, the
Maison Dorée, the Bains Chinois, the Grand Balcon . . . At
the corner of Rue de Richelieu, 'there was Frascati's, its name
religiously preserved by a café, a rival to that of the Cardinal
which faces it'. Frascati had been a famous gambling house,
closed in 1836 ('Vestal of love, from old Frascati's rooms' writes
Baudelaire in *The Little Old Ladies*). Buisson, a tailor but also an

entrepreneur, had built a luxury edifice in its place, where Balzac, as we have seen, had a pied-à-terre when he lived at Les Jardies. In return for his rent and his clothing, payment of which was irregular to say the least, he wrote in *The Lesser Bourgeoisie*: 'All Paris has seen one of its most famous tailors build at his own expense on the famous site of Frascati the most sumptuous construction.'

Across the street: 'What an attraction, what a heady atmosphere sparkles between Rue Taitbout and Rue de Richelieu!' Where Rue Taitbout approaches the boulevard, it was framed by two cafés: on the left the Café de Paris, and on the right Tortoni, whose porch was one of the most famous places in Paris, not to say the world. 'One leaves the battlefield of the Bourse to go to the restaurants, passing from one digestion to another. Isn't Tortoni both the preface and the denouement of the Bourse?' The dandies in *The Human Comedy* are all regulars at Tortoni. *Béatrix* presents three of the least commendable among them:

About one o'clock, Maxime [de Trailles] was chewing a toothpick and talking with Du Tillet on Tortoni's portico, where speculation held a little Bourse, a sort of prelude to the great one. He seemed to be engaged in business, but he was really awaiting Comte de La Palferine who, within a given time, was certain to pass that way. The Boulevard des Italiens is today what the Pont-Neuf was in 1650; all persons known to fame pass along it once, at least, in the course of the day. Accordingly, at the end of about ten minutes, Maxime dropped Du Tillet's arm, and nodding to the young prince of Bohemia said, smiling: 'One word with you, count.' The two rivals in their own principality, the one orb on his decline, the other like the rising sun, sat down upon four chairs before the Café de Paris.[80]

Just a stone's throw from Tortoni was the Opéra of that time, its entrance on Rue Le Peletier but directly connected to Boulevard des Italiens by the Passage de l'Opéra.[81] In *The Human Comedy*, many striking episodes take place at the Opéra, such as the flamboyant opening of *A Harlot High and Low*, the masked ball attended by Lucien de Rubempré, Vautrin, Rastignac, and the poor Esther (the 'Torpedo') who is horrified at being recognized and mocked by Bixiou, Lousteau, Lupeaux, Blondet, and co.

A little further on, on Boulevard Montmartre, the Variétés theatre nestled against the threshold of the Passage des Panoramas – between two large rotundas that offered panoramic views of the great cities of France and elsewhere. It these that gave rise to the fashion for what were then called *ramas*. At the Pension Vauquer, 'he makes a famous *froitorama*!' says Vautrin. And Bianchon corrects him: 'Illustrious Monsieur Vautrin, why do you say *froitorama*? That's mistaken, it's *froidorama*.' The Panoramas is the passage most frequently encountered in *The Human Comedy*. The Princesse de Cadignan tells how she met Michel Chrestien: 'The evening before the funeral of General Lamarque, I had gone out on foot with my son, and my republican accompanied us, sometimes behind, sometimes in front, from the Madeleine to the Passage des Panoramas, where I was going.' Balzac says no more: the Passages were for him ordinary ways, both the Panoramas and the Passage Vivienne where Godefroid, the Initiate, buys an accordion, or the Passage de l'Opéra, where 'the prince of Bohemia', La Palférine, challenges to a duel a pedestrian who has pushed him around. Whatever devotees of Walter Benjamin may say, these Parisian arcades were no more important to Balzac than any other street. Their poetry and evocative power date from the twentieth century, under the particular influence of the surrealists, who frequented the Passage de l'Opéra in the early 1920s:[82]

> From Rue Montmartre to Rue Saint-Denis, the boulevard's physiognomy changes completely . . . The Babylonian construction of the Pont de Fer, with its erroneous use of stucco; the Gymnase with its small, coquettish facade; further on, the Bonne-Nouvelle bazaar, as beautiful as a Venetian palace, arisen from the ground as if with the wave of a fairy's wand: all this is completely in vain, a waste of effort! There is no more elegance among the passers-by; fine dresses are almost out of place here; the artist and the literary lion no longer venture into these parts. The inelegant and provincial masses, in commerce and badly shod, arrive from Rue Saint-Denis, the faubourgs of the Temple and Rue Saint-Martin; the old proprietors, retired bourgeois, show themselves; and it is a whole other world.[83]

Then, from the Porte Saint-Martin, we have 'the people's Boulevard des Italiens . . . Eight theatres constantly attract their spectators here'. Balzac had adaptations of his novels performed in several of them, *The Wild Ass's Skin* at the Ambigu Comique, *Paméla Giraud* and *History of the Thirteen* at the Gaîté, *Colonel Chabert* and *Cousin Bette* at the Vaudeville, but we do not find in *The Human Comedy* the term 'Boulevard du Crime', which came into use only later, probably thanks to Marcel Carné's *Les Enfants du Paradis*. This section, which today corresponds to Boulevard Saint-Martin and Boulevard du Temple, was 'the only point in Paris where you can see the people swarming, rags to astonish a painter, and looks to frighten a bourgeois!'

Further on, bordering the Marais, begin 'deserted boulevards, without pedestrians, the wild moors of this royal promenade. Boredom seizes you there, the atmosphere of factories can be felt from afar. The pensioner walks here in his dressing gown, if he wants; and on fine days you can see blind people playing cards. *In piscem desinit elegantia.*'

But the walk does not end on this sad note:

> Beyond this, Boulevard Bourdon is no longer Paris: it is the countryside, it is the suburb, it is the highway, it is the majesty of nothingness; but it is one of the most magnificent places in Paris, the view is stunning. It is a Roman splendour without spectators! The Pont d'Austerlitz, the Seine at its widest point, Notre-Dame, the Jardin des Plantes, the Halle aux Vins, the Île Saint-Louis, the warehouses, the July column, the Bastille moat, the Salpêtrière, the Panthéon, everything is grandiose. Truly, the end of the Parisian drama is worthy of its beginning.[84]

New Paris: from the eastern faubourgs to the Champs-Élysées

At the time when Balzac was working on *Cromwell* – five acts in verse – in his garret on Rue Lesdiguières, the area between the boulevards and the city wall was still largely rural. It was here, in what corresponds to the present IXth arrondissement and part of the VIIIth, that the bulk of the new Paris developed under the Restoration and the July Monarchy. But it did not start from scratch. At the end of the Ancien Régime, two districts had already grown beyond the old Parisian boundary formed by the boulevards: the Faubourg Saint-Honoré and the Chaussée-d'Antin.[85]

The Faubourg Saint-Honoré was the older of the pair. It began to be built during the Regency period, when John Law's system provided a flow of money for speculators and developers –

ephemeral, like the system itself. Great lords built there, starting with the Comte d'Evreux, governor of the Île-de-France; his mansion was bought by Madame de Pompadour, who obtained permission from Louis XV to enlarge it by encroaching on the Champs-Élysées to plant a vegetable garden.[86] The lord chancellor d'Aguesseau, the Duc de Charost, the farmer-general Grimod de la Reynière, father of the famous gastronome – a regular at the Rocher de Cancale – built their mansions in the Faubourg Saint-Honoré, many of which are still standing.

In *The Human Comedy*, this faubourg is as noble as the Faubourg Saint-Germain, but not of the same level: the families are less ancient, less famous than the Grandlieus, the Beauséants, or the Blamont-Chevrys. We meet rich foreigners there, including Fœdora, Raphaël's icy love in *The Wild Ass's Skin*:

> I returned on foot from the Faubourg Saint-Honoré where Fœdora lived. Almost the entire length of Paris stretches between her mansion and Rue des Cordiers; even though it was a raw night, it seemed a short way to me. What a crazy idea! To set out to conquer Fœdora, in winter – a hard one – when my worldly possessions amounted to less than thirty francs, when the distance between us was so great![87]

Fœdora was indeed a countess, but of Russian origin, and nothing was known of her family.

Balzac himself frequented the brilliant salon of Princesse Belgioso, on Rue d'Anjou. He had this rich Milanese emigrant read *La Chartreuse de Parme*, as he 'found in the Princess B*** some traits of the Sanseverina'.[88] We also meet him at the home of Princesse Bagration, widow of a Russian general killed at Borodino, a famous beauty who entertained in the Hôtel de

Brunoy, and who may have served as a model for the character of Fœdora – something Balzac denied.[89] 'You want to know,' he wrote to Madame Hanska, 'if I have met Fœdora, if she is real? A woman from cold Russia, the Princesse Bagration, is seen in Paris as the model. Sixty-two women have already been impertinent enough to recognize themselves in her. They are all of a mature age. Madame Récamier herself wanted to *fœdoriser* herself. None of this is true.'[90]

Some salons in the Faubourg Saint-Honoré were open to liberals (in the sense of 1825), such as that of Destutt de Tracy, where Benjamin Constant, Stendhal and La Fayette met. Elsewhere, bankers, industrialists, visiting foreigners and artists crossed paths. Introduced to Fœdora's salon for the first time by Rastignac, Raphaël met 'scholars, men of letters, former ministers, peers of France'.[91] Through this mixture, the Faubourg Saint-Honoré appears as an intermediary between the stiff Faubourg Saint-Germain and the complaisant Chaussée-d'Antin.

The beginnings of the Chaussée-d'Antin date from the 1770s, after speculation on ecclesiastical land such as the 'Mathurins' marsh', located between what was to become Rue de la Chaussée-d'Antin and Rue Taitbout. Here the greatest architects of the time built primarily for two categories of clients, linked in many ways: bankers and actresses. Brongniart, the architect of the Bourse and designer of Père-Lachaise, built the Hôtel Radix de Sainte-Foix, at the corner of Rue de la Chaussée-d'Antin and Boulevard des Italiens, with a hanging garden above Rue Basse-du-Rempart. Bélanger, the architect of the Château de Bagatelle, built for Mademoiselle Dervieux, a famous dancer and actress, a small hôtel with a large garden on

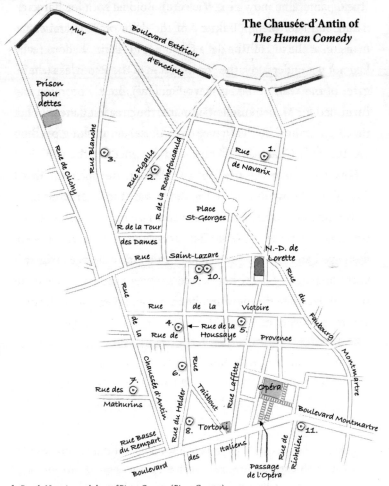

The Chausée-d'Antin of *The Human Comedy*

1. Rue de Navarin: workshop of Pierre Grassou (*Pierre Grassou*)
2. Rue Pigalle: Florine's apartment (*A Daughter of Eve*)
3. Rue Blanche: Jenny Cadine's apartment (*Béatrix*)
4. Rue du Houssaye: office of the Keller bank
5. Rue de la Victoire [formerly Chantereine]: office of the Mongenod bank
6. Rue Taitbout: Esther's apartment (*A Harlot High and Low*)
7. Rue des Mathurins [or Rue Neuve-des-Mathurins]: Du Tillet's mansion (*A Daughter of Eve*)
8. Rue du Helder: the mansion of Mme de Restaud, daughter of Old Goriot
9. Rue Saint-Lazare: the mansion of the Baron de Nucingen and his wife Delphine
10. Rue Saint-Lazare: the Hôtel San-Réal (*The Girl with the Golden Eyes*)
11. The Buisson building, on the site of Frascati's, Balzac's pied-à-terre when he lived in Les Jardies

Rue Chantereine (now de la Victoire). Boullée built for Baron de Thun, minister plenipotentiary of the duke of Wurtemberg, a mansion at the top of Rue de la Chaussée-d'Antin. Ledoux, who had not yet undertaken the construction of the Propylées (the 57 gates of the Wall of the Farmers-General), built, decorated and furnished for Mademoiselle Guimard, the greatest dancer of her time (maintained by the Prince de Soubise), a ravishing pavilion on Rue de la Chaussée-d'Antin, and designed for the widow of a Geneva banker the pearl of the district, the splendid Hôtel Thélusson, between Rue de Provence and Rue Chantereine.

By the time Balzac wrote *The Human Comedy*, almost nothing remained of these marvels. The mansions with gardens were destroyed and the land subdivided to build residences that still bore the name of *hôtel*, but lacked grandeur either in size or in style. Balzac saw this new architecture as a reflection of the prevailing mediocrity:

> If the axiom that architecture is the expression of manners and morals was ever proved, was it not after the insurrection of 1830, during the present reign of the house of Orleans? As all the old fortunes are diminishing in France, the majestic mansions of our ancestors are constantly being demolished and replaced by species of phalansteries, in which the peers of July occupy the third floor above some newly enriched Empire men on the lower floors. A mixture of styles is confusedly employed. As there is no longer a real court or nobility to give the tone, there is no harmony in the production of art. Never, on the other hand, has architecture discovered so many economical ways of imitating the real and the solid, or displayed more resources, more talent, in distributing them.[92]

The first time Rastignac visits Delphine de Nucingen in her mansion on Rue Saint-Lazare, he discovers 'one of those

frivolous houses, with slim columns and scanty porticoes –
which pass for handsome in Paris – a typical banker's house, full
of expensive, affected elegance, with stucco, and marble mosaic
landings. He found Madame de Nucingen in a small drawing
room painted in the Italian style, whose décor resembled that of
a café.'[93] To top it all, these 'wretched' buildings that Balzac so
despised have also been destroyed since his time, so that the
Chaussée d'Antin district now has little charm except in the eyes
of children admiring the windows of Galeries Lafayette at
Christmas time.

Of all the Balzac neighbourhoods, the Chaussée-d'Antin is
the richest in characters, encounters, and various adventures.
Unlike the Faubourg Saint-Germain or the Marais, this district,
which is open to the city centre, became the fashionable place to
be from the July Revolution onwards, between Boulevard des
Italiens and Rue Saint-Lazare and, in the other direction, from
Rue Taitbout to Rue Caumartin. It was populated by the rich.
The Duc de Navarreins and the Duc de Granlieu chat at the
bedside of the Duchesse de Langeais:

> Her son, Marigny, is an amiable man . . . The other day he was
> dining at the Cercle the other day with all that rich set from the
> Chaussée-d'Antin, and your uncle (who always goes there for his
> card game) saw him. Astonished to meet him there, he asks him if
> he is part of the Cercle. 'Yes, I do not go only into society now, I
> live among bankers.'[94]

The uncle's astonishment is understandable: members of the high
nobility do not frequent the Chaussée-d'Antin – with rare exceptions, such as the case of Madame de Sérisy, Lucien de Rubempré's
lover, whom she stole from the Duchesse de Maufrigneuse. She

lives on Rue de la Chaussée-d'Antin and is noble, but not quite noble enough to be received by the Grandlieu family.

Old Goriot's two daughters live in the same neighbourhood, Madame de Restaud on Rue du Helder and Delphine de Nucingen on Rue Saint-Lazare. Delphine is very quickly interested in Rastignac, not only because he is charming, but also because he is the cousin of a great lady, Madame de Beauséant, and she hopes to be accepted by the Faubourg Saint-Germain thanks to him. Madame de Beauséant explains the world to her young cousin:

> The beautiful Madame Delphine de Nucingen, the wife of a money-man, is dying of pique; she's consumed by jealousy, she's a thousand leagues behind her sister; her sister is no longer her sister; the two women disown each other just as each disowns her father. And that's why Madame de Nucingen would lap up all the mud that lies between Rue Saint-Lazare and Rue de Grenelle to enter my drawing room.[95]

Nucingen is not the only 'money man' in the Chaussée-d'Antin: all the bankers in *The Human Comedy* are there: Keller on Rue du Houssaye, Du Tillet on Rue de la Chaussée-d'Antin, Mongenod on Rue Chantereine (now de la Victoire).[96] And power goes hand in hand with money, as Blondet explains to Raphaël in *The Wild Ass's Skin*:

> The infamous monarchy which has been overthrown by popular heroism was a woman of loose life with whom one could banquet and make merry; but our country itself is a virtuous – not to say shrewish – spouse. We must, whether we will or not, put up with her frigid caresses. So here we are: political power has moved from the Tuileries Palace to the newspaper offices, just as economic

power has changed its address from the Faubourg Saint-Germain to the Chaussée-d'Antin.[97]

In *The Human Comedy*, Rue Taitbout, which Louis Chevalier sees as the most Balzacian street in Paris, is the street of happy love. The hero of *A Second Home*, Roger, extracts the beautiful Caroline from the darkness of Rue du Tourniquet-Saint-Jean and installs her on Rue Taitbout, in one of those apartments 'that seem made on purpose for newly-married couples to spend their honeymoon . . . a house whose stone walls were still white, where the columns of the hall and the doorway were as yet spotless, and the inner walls shone with the neat painting which our recent intimacy with English ways had brought into fashion'.[98] In *A Harlot High and Low*, the Abbé Herrera (Vautrin) buys an apartment on Rue Taitbout for Esther, who is able to leave the horrible Rue de Langlade, as we have seen, and settle down with her Lucien for a brief moment of happiness.

Balzac had friends in the Chaussée-d'Antin: Berlioz on Rue de Provence (Balzac lent him a coat for a trip to Russia), Eugène Sue on Rue Caumartin, Alexandre Dumas, then George Sand and Chopin on the Square d'Orléans, at the top of Rue Taitbout.[99] However, the Square d'Orléans is not quite the Chaussée d'Antin. Once you cross Rue Saint-Lazare, you enter what is really the 'second Paris': a circle of *quartiers* built around 1825 that form a satellite ring around the Chaussée: Nouvelle Athènes, Notre-Dame-de-Lorette, Saint-Georges and, further west, the Europe quarter.

No doubt linked to the philhellenism of the 1820s, the name Nouvelle Athènes (which does not appear in *The Human Comedy*) refers to a small housing development between Rue Saint-Lazare, Rue Blanche, Rue de la Tour-des-Dames, and Rue de

La Rochefoucauld. Here we meet the great characters of Parisian Romanticism: theatre people such as Talma, Mademoiselle Mars and Mademoiselle Duchesnois on Rue de la Tour-des-Dames, writers, painters, musicians . . . It is here, on Rue Blanche, that Fabien du Ronceret had a 'delightful garden apartment' arranged for the pretty Madame Cadine, designed by Grindot, the architect omnipresent in *The Human Comedy*, and decorated by Léon de Lora.

The church of Notre-Dame-de-Lorette, begun under Charles X and completed under Louis-Philippe at the time of publication of *Old Man Goriot*, gave its name to the neighbourhood surrounding it, between Rue Saint-Georges and Faubourg Montmartre, but it also came to designate its most attractive population, the *lorettes*. The first sentence of *A Man of Business*, dedicated to Baron James de Rothschild, runs:

> The word *lorette* is a euphemism invented to describe the status of a personage, or a personage of a status, of which it is awkward to speak; the French Académie, in its modesty, having omitted to supply a definition out of regard for the age of its forty members. Whenever a new word comes to supply the place of an unwieldy circumlocution its fortune is assured.

The paternity of the word was however debated. 'Gavarni', wrote Baudelaire,

> created the Lorette. She existed, indeed, a little before his time, but he completed her. I even believe it was he who invented the word. The Lorette . . . is not the same thing as the 'kept woman', that feature of the Empire, condemned to live in funereal intimacy with the clinking corpse – a general or a banker – on which she depended. The Lorette is a free agent. She comes and she goes.

She keeps open house. She is no one's mistress; she consorts with the artists and the journalists. She does what she can to be witty.[100]

In *The Human Comedy*, many *lorettes* live in the neighbourhood around the church, but also a little further north in the Saint-Georges quarter, which extends around the square of the same name, 'the Faubourg Saint-Germain of the XIIIth arrondissement'.[101] The actress Florine, the horsewoman Malaga, the dancer Mariette, Olympia Bijou, Tullia, Euphrasie, Antonia, Madame du Val-Noble, Carabine, Héloïse Brisetout . . . They

pass through Paris like gossamer through the atmosphere, without our knowing where they go nor whence they came; today queens, tomorrow slaves . . . in short, that whole exceptional feminine society, so kindly, so graceful in its easy 'sans-souci', which absorbs into its own Bohemian life all who allow themselves to be caught in the frantic whirl of its gay spirits, its eager abandonment, and its contemptuous indifference to the future.[102]

Balzac shows that this 'exceptional feminine society' is close to his heart. He loves, esteems, and respects the young women he has created, whereas the noble ladies of high society are either seductive, egotistical, and brutal (Antoinette de Langeais, Diane de Maufrigneuse, Fœdora, Béatrix de Rochefide), or else more or less virtuous dimwits.[103] Balzac's *lorettes*, on the other hand, form a kindly society. For those they love they are capable of devotion, even self-sacrifice. In *A Daughter of Eve*, the beautiful Florine lodges and feeds Raoul Nathan, a specimen of journalistic bohemia. He is rarely at home, 'on the third floor of an ugly and narrow house . . . a poor enough lodging, cold and bare', in a passage between Rue du Rempart and Rue Neuve-des-Mathurins (now Rue des Mathurins):

His real home, his fine existence, his presentation of himself before his friends, was in the house of Mademoiselle Florine . . . For ten years Raoul had attached himself so closely to this woman that he passed more than half his life with her; he took all his meals at her house unless he had some friend to invite, or an invitation to dinner elsewhere.[104]

When Nathan, though penniless, decided to start a newspaper, Florine sold everything she owned – furniture, paintings, jewellery – and got seventy thousand francs, which she entrusted to her lover. 'Five days later she gave a splendid feast. The new journal was baptized in floods of wine and wit, with oaths of loyalty, fidelity, and good fellowship.'

Nothing better reveals Balzac's feelings towards his favourite creations than the fates of three heroines: Coralie, Esther, and Josépha (all Jews, which is curious – did he know so many, or is this more of an Orientalist fantasy?). 'The Jews, though so often debased by their contact with other peoples, yet present among their various tribes strains in which this sublimest type of Asiatic beauty is preserved.'[105]

Coralie, seeing her Lucien ruined as a result of dubious journalistic manoeuvres, sold all her furniture, left her beautiful flat on Rue de Vendôme (now Rue Béranger) and moved 'into a little three-roomed flat on the fourth floor of a house on Rue de la Lune, close to the Gymnase. There Coralie was waiting for Lucien. All she had saved from the wreck was her unsullied love and a modest sum of twelve hundred francs.'[106] Very quickly, illness followed misery and she died; at the wake, Lucien, in tears, composed the songs that would pay for her coffin.

Later, in *A Harlot High and Low*, Esther's love for Lucien – who is undoubtedly a woman's darling despite all his faults – leads

Coralie (Nanteuil,
Édition Furne)

her to endure all the miseries imposed on her by the terrible Carlos Herrera (Vautrin): she converts to Catholicism and enters a convent; then, finding her lover, she only agrees to see him withdrawn from the world; she comes to terms with the fact that Lucien must marry Clotilde de Grandlieu; and, finally, Carlos persuades her to give in to the advances of Baron de Nucingen, who has met her one night in the Bois de Vincennes, in order to save Lucien – but, at the moment of concluding the deal, she kills herself by swallowing poison.

Josépha Mirah, 'prima donna of the Royal Academy of Music' and former mistress of Baron Hulot, is visited one day by his wife, who is trying to trace the missing baron. Waiting in a salon decorated in 'purple and gold silk', she prepares herself for a humiliating reception:

> The Baroness . . . had been hoping to see Josépha the fascinating man-eater, the opera singer, the dazzling and voluptuous courtesan; and she had found a serene and well-poised woman, with the noble dignity given to her by her talent, the simplicity of an actress who knows that every evening she is a queen; and, even more unexpectedly, a courtesan who in her looks, her attitude and manner, was paying full and unreserved homage to the virtuous wife, to the *Mater dolorosa* of the holy hymn, and making an offering of flowers to her sorrows, as in Italy they adorn the Madonna.
>
> 'Madame,' she said, in a tone of profound humility, 'I wronged you before I knew you; but now that I have had the good fortune to behold in you the most perfect image of virtue that exists on earth, believe me I know how great my fault was, and do sincerely repent it, and you may count on my doing the utmost to repair it!'[107]

A magnificent symbolic interview, in which generosity and nobility of soul are clearly on the side of the *lorette*.

Balzac's courtesans have many traits in common with their creator: disregard for rules, imagination, heedlessness of risk, a sense of the magical. They resemble the man who 'often observed in himself the numerous types that live in his work'.[108]

The Quartier de l'Europe, which extended the satellite ring of the Chaussée d'Antin to the west, was built from 1825 onwards, but its beginnings were slow owing to the commercial and financial crisis that hit the country after starting in Great Britain. So much so that in 1835, when the action of *Béatrix* takes place, the district was still under construction:

Without the Aspasias of the Notre-Dame-de-Lorette quarter, far fewer houses would be built in Paris. Pioneers in fresh stucco, they have gone, towed by speculation, along the heights of Montmartre, pitching their tents in those solitudes of carved free-stone, the like of which adorns the streets named after Amsterdam, Milan, Stockholm, London and Moscow in the Quartier de l'Europe, architectural steppes where the wind rustles innumerable papers on which a void is divulged by the words, 'Apartments to let.' The situation of these dames is determined by that which they take in the apocryphal regions. If their house is near the line traced by Rue de Provence, the woman has an income, her budget prospers; but if she approaches the farther line of the outer boulevards or rises towards the horrid town of Batignolles, she is without resources. When Monsieur de Rochefide first encountered Madame Schontz, she lived on the third floor of the only house that remained on Rue de Berlin; thus she was camping on the border-land between misery and its reverse.[109]

Thanks to Monsieur de Rochefide, Madame Schontz moved to a more up-market neighbourhood: he established her in an apartment on Rue Neuve-Saint-Georges and then in a house on Rue La Bruyère.

To the west of the Quartier de l'Europe, once you cross Rue d'Amsterdam, you enter an island of dirt and misery, Petite Pologne. There are no Poles here – the name comes from a tavern dating back to the reign of Louis XV – only tramps, ragpickers, and scavengers. This small triangle bounded by Rue du Rocher, Rue de la Pépinière, and Rue de Miromesnil – in the middle of which the church of Saint-Augustin now stands – is described by Pique-Vinaigre in Eugène Sue's *Les Mystères de Paris*:

A notorious den for the underworld; there were no streets, only alleys; no houses, only hovels; no pavement, only a small carpet of

mud and manure, which meant that the noise of carts would not
have bothered you, as none passed that way. From morning till
night, and especially from night till morning, the only thing you
could hear was the cries of 'Help!' or 'Murder!' The more people
in Little Poland were stupefied by drink, the fewer people there
were to arrest.[110]

At the end of *Cousin Bette*, Baron Hulot, who has fallen through
a series of liaisons to the depths of decay, lives in this 'branch of
the Faubourg Saint-Marceau' with an eighteen-year-old girl,
and it is there that Baroness Hulot, who does charitable work in
the neighbourhood, finally finds him.

The destruction of Petite Pologne began under the July monarchy: 'At this moment,' Balzac wrote, 'speculation, which
seeks to change the face of this corner of Paris and build on
the wasteland that separates Rue d'Amsterdam from Rue du
Faubourg-du-Roule, will undoubtedly modify the population,
for the trowel is, in Paris, more civilizing than one might
think!'[111] This change would take time: Manet found his model
for *The Old Musician* in La Petite Pologne, not far from his
studio on Rue Médéric.

On the far side of this enclosure of misery, the Parc Monceau
quarter appears in *The Human Comedy* as a place of retreat for
women who have experienced the glory of the social world.
Diane de Maufrigneuse, who became Princesse de Cadignan
'after the disasters of the July Revolution, which destroyed
several aristocratic fortunes dependent on the court . . . very
wisely decided to live in retirement, and to make herself, if possible, forgotten'.[112] She lived on Rue de Miromesnil, 'in the
modestly priced ground floor of a small hôtel':

When one thinks of what the beautiful Duchesse de Maufrigneuse
had been under the Restoration – one of the queens of Paris, a
dazzling queen, whose luxurious existence equalled that of the
richest women of fashion in London – there was something touching in the sight of her in that humble little abode on Rue de
Miromesnil, a few steps away from her splendid mansion, which no
amount of fortune had enabled her to keep, and which the hammer
of speculators has since demolished.[113]

It is in this humble shell that the beautiful love story between the
princess and d'Arthez, the great writer intoxicated by 'the greatest actress of the day', takes place.

For her part, at the end of *Béatrix*, Madame de Rochefide
explains to Calyste, who is now married but still loves her: 'I am
hidden in Rue de Chartres opposite the Parc de Monceau, in a
little house suitable to my means; and there I cram my head with
literature – but only for myself, to distract my thoughts.' Having
run away and left her fortune to her husband, she 'had gone to
the summit of the hill on which lies the Parc de Monceaux, and
there she had taken refuge in a "little house" formerly belonging
to a great seigneur, standing on the street, but possessed of a
charming garden, the rent of which did not exceed eighteen
hundred francs.'[114] For these women who had withdrawn from
the world, it was no longer magnificence, but these 'small hôtels'
still had a certain luxury, even if less than that of the neighbouring faubourg.

Further west, we enter a region that was still almost rural
during Balzac's youth, with marshes and meadows. Only the
lower part of the Champs-Élysées was built on, and still not con-
tinuously. The large central avenue was the place for horse and

carriage rides, where people went to be seen and admired. Lucien
de Rubempré was penniless after being abandoned by Madame
de Bargeton:

> Lost in thought, he walked straight forward, gazing at the monu-
> ments in the Place Louis XV [now de la Concorde]. It was a fine
> day. Fine carriages were constantly passing to and fro before his
> eyes as he made for the Grand Avenue of the Champs-Élysées. He
> followed the crowd of strollers and thus he saw the three or four
> thousand carriages which, on any fine Sunday, flow along this
> avenue and constitute a sort of impromptu Longchamp procession.
> Dazzled by the splendour of the horses, clothes and liveries, he
> went on and on until he arrived in front of the unfinished
> Arc-de-Triomphe. What were his thoughts when, on the way
> back, he saw Madame d'Espard and Madame de Bargeton in an
> admirable four-wheeled turn-out, behind which waved the plumes
> of the footmen whose gold-embroidered green coat enabled Lucien
> to recognize the two ladies . . . Young men on horseback, among
> whom Lucien could distinguish de Marsay and Rastignac, joined
> the barouche to escort the two cousins to the Bois de Boulogne.[115]

The Allée des Veuves, today the luxurious and vulgar Avenue
Montaigne, is still an unsafe place at its end, near the Seine. It is
there that, in *Les Mystères de Paris*, Rodolphe nearly gets drowned
at the Coeur-Saignant by rising waters: he 'had not noticed one
of those underground taverns which, until a few years ago, were
to be seen in certain parts of the Champs-Élysées and especially
near the Cours-la-Reine. A staircase dug into the earth led to the
bottom of a kind of wide ditch; on one of its sides, cut steeply,
leaned a low, squalid, cracked hovel.'[116] Rodolphe was saved in
extremis from drowning by the Chourineur. In 1830, Victor
Hugo was almost adventurous when he settled on Rue Jean-
Goujon, a stone's throw from the Allée des Veuves, in the only

house built in the neighbourhood. But about fifteen years later, the Bal Mabille opened on this avenue, and quickly became a fashionable place. Parties were held in the evenings, as the whole area was lit by gas. 'The bushes were filled with tinted glass globes, girandoles were planted, lines of lampposts and even, to top it all, steel palms with torches on their branches. These ornaments were supposed to produce a magical effect at nightfall.'[117] At the Bal Mabille, one could meet Rambouteau, the prefect of Paris, as well as Théophile Gautier, Alexandre Dumas, Eugène Sue, and even Balzac himself. In *Cousin Bette*, Josépha says to Baron Hulot: 'That will make up for the unhappiness you have caused in your own home. You will be redeeming your sins, and having a good time like a tart [*lorette*] at Mabille.'[118]

So much so that in 1845, Balzac could conclude his *Histoire et physiologie des boulevards de Paris* with this prediction:

> A formidable competition is being prepared against the boulevards. Today, distinguished people promenade on the Champs-Élysées, on the southern sidewalk; but the same impediment that makes the boulevards impassable in rainy weather, the most frequent weather in Paris, will for a long time stop the success of the great Avenue des Champs-Élysées.[119]

And it was towards the top of the Champs-Élysées, on a street under construction in the Beaujon district, that Balzac, after much searching, at last found his final home.

The Press

From *The Chouans* (1829) to *Cousin Bette* (1846), the years of Balzac's great creation coincided with upheavals in the press: the periodicals inherited from the eighteenth century gave way to newspapers as modern as those in London. Balzac was both a witness to and a key player in this paper revolution, and it can even be said that for at least a year around 1830 he was a fully fledged journalist.[1]

What drove him to this conversion was the need for money. At the end of the Restoration, the 'book trade' (what we now call publishing) was in a very bad way for many reasons: production and distribution were archaic, credit was unorganized and, above all, the network of reading rooms throughout the country led to a reduction in print runs, the fragmentation of works into two or three volumes, and an increase in prices. High prices encouraged counterfeiting by Belgian booksellers, who flooded the market with the same titles as in Paris, presented in a single compact volume and much cheaper.

This crisis in the book trade mainly affected publishers of novels: there were hardly any major publishers of this kind who did not go bankrupt at some point.[2] Print runs were low and royalties, calculated on the basis of print runs rather than sales, remained miserable. Balzac could rightly write at one point: 'During the years 28, 29 and 30, I did not earn more than 3,000 fr.'[3]

In the first years he spent on Rue Cassini, he was penniless. On 5 October 1831, he wrote to his sister Laure: 'My dear sister, I have found a way to postpone my payment until the 13th, and by then I will have enough money to cover my needs; but, in order not to have to go begging, I ask you to lend me about twenty francs, which you can give to Flore.'[4] Not only does he need money for current expenses, he has to pay the enormous debts linked to the bankruptcy of the printing house on Rue des Marais. As novels did not pay, he decided to try journalism – the turn that Lousteau would describe in *Lost Illusions*:

> The little money my family was able to give me was soon used up. I found myself penniless after getting a play accepted to the Théâtre-Français . . . Where, how and by what shifts was I to earn my daily bread? That was the problem which the pangs of hunger forced me to face. After many attempts, after writing an anonymous novel for which Doguereau – he didn't make much out of it – paid me two hundred francs, I plainly saw that I could only live by journalism.[5]

In the meantime, Balzac wrote to Charles Sédillot (his mother's cousin by marriage, in charge of the liquidation of his business):

My dear cousin, if I have not been to see you about the Mame note, attribute the reason for this only to the necessity by which I have, at the moment, to spend my days and nights working to provide for the daily needs of life. The bookshops are dead. My only resource lies in newspapers, and I barely have time to meet their demands.[6]

Rather than become a freelance with the daily press, which was rather poor in the field of culture, Balzac turned to periodicals, particularly as he had had a decisive encounter in 1829 with Émile de Girardin. At only twenty-five years of age, Girardin was already at the head of successful publishing businesses. The previous year he had founded *Le Voleur*, which, as its name suggests and thanks to the weak copyright protection, consisted mainly of fragments stolen from other newspapers. In 1829, he founded *La Mode*, a weekly aimed at women, but which soon became the journal of elegant society. Balzac collaborated on these two periodicals, and his relationship with Girardin became so close that in February 1830 they founded a company for the publication of the *Feuilleton des Journaux Politiques*, devoted to the book trade. Balzac also sent texts to *La Silhouette*, a newspaper that embarked on caricature under the impetus of Philipon and Henri Monnier, with the financial support of Girardin.

Balzac's income from these collaborations was meagre – Girardin once wrote to him: 'I would be forced to give up your collaboration if your demands were higher than 40 centimes a line' – but the huge advantage was that journals paid in cash and not with promissory notes.[7]

We may wonder how Girardin and Balzac managed to run journals with such divergent political orientations: *Le Voleur* was cautiously opposed to the Polignac ministry and oriented to a liberal succession; *La Mode*, rather aristocratic, was under the patronage of the Duchesse de Berry; the *Feuilleton des Journaux Politiques* counted among its collaborators Saint-Simonians who were disciples of Buchez, while *La Silhouette* was almost openly republican. Balzac was careful not to take a position and remained politically neutral during and after the great upheaval of the July Revolution.

The change of regime aggravated the contradictions between Girardin's publications, but he knew how to manoeuvre skilfully: '*La Mode*,' he said, 'is less a newspaper than a forum where all opinions can be represented and debated.'[8] He let *La Feuilleton* capsize following dissensions among the Saint-Simonians; as for *La Silhouette*, it disappeared after 1830, replaced by *La Caricature*, in which Girardin was no longer involved. Philipon now took the helm, publishing the famous pear-shaped portraits of Louis-Philippe, but it was Balzac who wrote the *Prospectus* at the head of the first issue (and in fact the entire issue): 'The arts have very little to expect from the government, and only the people will know how to remunerate them magnificently' – an indication of a cautious and hesitant opposition, by no means republican.

Often anonymous or signed with fancy names, Balzac's contributions to these various publications form a tangled web from which a few outstanding texts emerge.[9]

In the *Feuilleton des Journaux Politiques*, Balzac wrote *De l'État actuel de la librairie*, in which he analysed the weaknesses of the current system: sales on credit and what was for him the 'real plague', the fragmentation of the book trade:

> Booksellers are divided into three classes: 1) publisher-booksellers who buy manuscripts, or reprint old authors, and make these into

books; 2) dealer-booksellers and retail booksellers, to whom the former deliver considerable parts of their product; 3) provincial or Parisian booksellers who put themselves in communication with the buyer. This absurd hierarchy, whose purpose is to make a book pay three taxes before it reaches the public, is the cause of all the misfortunes of this deplorable trade.

And Balzac proposes a solution:

The salvation of the book trade and its restoration depend on very little. It is a question of forcing someone who gets a book printed to pay the author, the printer and the paper-maker, and to sell the work to the public himself, without making him bear three ransoms. Finally, it is necessary for a volume to be manufactured exactly like a loaf of bread, and be sold like a loaf of bread, with no other intermediary than the bookseller between author and consumer.[10]

Like Diderot in his *Lettre sur le commerce de la librairie*, Balzac touches on points that remain relevant today.

In *La Silhouette*, he published 'Des Artistes', a plea for the freedom of creators, which ends with the following words:

Savages and peoples who most closely resemble the state of nature are far greater in their relations with superior men than the most civilized nations. Among them, men with second sight, bards and improvisers are regarded as privileged creatures. Their artists have a place at the feast, are protected by all, their pleasures are respected, their sleep and their old age as well. This phenomenon is rare in a civilized nation, and more often than not when a light shines, people run to put it out because they think it is a fire.[11]

After the July Revolution, Balzac published in *La Mode* fragments that eventually led to the *Traité de la vie élégante*, organized into definitions and aphorisms – 'A man becomes rich, he is born elegant', or 'Dress consists less in clothing than in the manner of wearing it' – mixed with amusing anecdotes, such as an imaginary meeting with Beau Brummell. The *Traité* is an apologia for the aristocracy, a praise of idleness, of the 'desire not to belong to the suffering class'. As long as societies have existed, Balzac writes, 'government has always necessarily been an insurance contract between the rich and the poor'. Surreptitiously, the text appears as a critique of the austere mores and dull fashion that were the hallmarks of the new monarchy.

Between September 1830 and March 1831, Balzac published every ten days a series of *Lettres sur Paris* in *Le Voleur*, signed 'Le Voleur', and addressed to imaginary correspondents in various provincial towns. Paid 100 francs for three articles per month, these letters give a remarkable picture of France in the aftermath of the July Revolution. They deal with the most diverse subjects: the physiognomy of the Parisian street in September ('The elegant cabriolets, the carriages, the fashionable people drive or run as before; and except for a few less trees, the boulevards are still the same'); the rumours of war against the European coalition; the Saint-Simonians ('For some days we have had a little religion to laugh about'); the sacking of the archbishop's palace; the demonstrations calling for the trial of Charles X's ministers ('About midnight I found the Palais-Royal surrounded by numerous groups shouting: "Death to the former ministers!" The drama I had announced to you is beginning in the streets'); the battle over *Hernani* ('If M. Victor Hugo was punished for his temptation by a triumphal fall, there is in him the stuff of some masterpiece

that will make him forget it'); as well as notes on Byron and
Goethe, Paganini, and Taglioni. In the last letter, there was a
prediction that would indeed come true: 'The great drama finished, I have no doubt that we will have the little play in 1831;
as under the Directory, Frascati, Barras and his costumes came
after the Convention.'

Heine, a friend of Balzac's, may have remembered this joyful
mixture of politics and cultural life when he wrote his letters
from Paris to the *Augsbürger Zeitung* in 1832 and in the 1840s.[12]
But what is certain is that the political events mentioned in
Heine's Paris letters are absent from *The Human Comedy* – or if
mentioned at all, it is almost carelessly, in an aside. If Balzac does
not speak of them in his novels, it is by deliberate choice and not
by ignorance or oversight.

Just before the July Revolution, two literary journals which
were to play a major role for Balzac and the writers of his day
were launched at almost the same time. Dr Véron, a doctor who
had made his fortune with a pectoral creme, founded the *Revue
de Paris*, which appeared every Sunday in sixty-four pages. A
few months later, François Buloz, a former printer and proofreader, took control of a failing travel magazine that he would
raise to the heights: the *Revue des Deux Mondes*. (He would also
buy the *Revue de Paris* in 1834.) Very quickly, the success was
immense. The prospectus for the first issue of the *Revue des
Deux Mondes* in 1831 'could list the names of Balzac, Alexandre
Dumas, Victor Hugo, Loève-Veimars, Eugène Sue and Alfred
de Vigny. Nodier and Sainte-Beuve, who were present in the
summary for the first half of the year, very likely insisted on not
being named.'[13]

Balzac was immediately attracted to Buloz:

I don't know what fraternal impulse drew me to M. Buloz, ex-proof-reader as I was ex-printer. We often shared the modest, frugal dinners that I regularly took. Although the sheets of the *Revue des Deux Mondes* came to forty lines of exaggerated justification and fifty-six execrable letters, devouring the manuscript, and although at that time I was far from familiar with the language with which I was struggling, I first gave M. Buloz my sheets at one hundred or one hundred and twenty francs; he paid me one hundred and fifty francs for the last ones, after his efforts had brought subscribers back to the fold.[14]

In 1831, Balzac gave up the 'petty journalism' he had been doing for a year and resumed his work as a novelist. For him, magazines were both a means to launch his career and a way of earning a living at a time when the book trade was in the doldrums. He sometimes sent them short stories – to the *Revue des Deux Mondes*, he entrusted *Le Petit Souper*, a fantastic tale, and *The Hated Son*; to the *Revue de Paris*, *A Passion in the Desert* – and sometimes fragments that he took up again in the finished novels (fragments of *A Woman of Thirty* and *The Wild Ass's Skin* to the *Revue de Paris*). But the relationship with Buloz soon deteriorated seriously. Buloz had a poor opinion of Balzac, perhaps under the influence of the *Revue des Deux Mondes'* great critic, Sainte-Beuve, who was very hostile to the novelist. The two men had been at loggerheads since the publication of articles in both journals criticizing the *Contes drolatiques*. When Buloz suggested that they 'renew our old relations', Balzac replied: 'If you want to buy a few sheets of blackened paper that you have accustomed me to consider as a commodity, Madame de Balzac has my manuscripts and will tell you my conditions.'[15] Four years later, it was expected that Balzac would entrust Buloz with the manuscript of *The Lily in the Valley*. But, on 29 December 1835,

Buloz wrote to George Sand:

> I am falling out with Balzac, who is going to work on an obscure
> journal which has often treated you badly, *La Gazette de Paris*; I
> assure you that I do not regret Balzac, I have never been able to get
> on with him and I have little regard for his style, despite its being
> much appreciated by the public. What led to the quarrel was a
> misappropriation of proofs which was made during my trip to
> Nohant; but the real reason is that he wanted to publish *The Lily of
> the Valley* in the *Revue des Deux Mondes*, whereas I wanted it only
> for the *Revue de Paris*. What the hell! Balzac is too like Scudéry to
> suit the *Revue des Deux Mondes*, I respect the *Revue* too much. Will
> you not agree that I am right?[16]

The 'misappropriation of proofs' referred to by Buloz led to
an even more serious problem. The *Revue de Paris* had sent
proofs of *The Lily of the Valley*, uncorrected by Balzac, to a magazine in St Petersburg; the author, always anxious for perfection,
was furious and refused to deliver the rest of the manuscript.
Buloz wrote to him: 'If you interfere with the publication of
something for which you have received the price and which no
longer belongs to you, the *Revue* will take you to court.'[17] Indeed,
a court case followed, which Balzac won, but which marked the
end of his relationship with Buloz.[18]

This kind of setback no doubt explains the idea that then
germinated in Balzac's mind, of owning a journal of his own.
This plan led him to acquire *La Chronique de Paris*, a small political and literary sheet appearing on Sundays and Thursdays,
founded in 1834 by a journalist of Irish origin, William Duck-
ett, in association with a printer named Béthune. In December
1835, Balzac borrowed 45,000 francs from friends and his
brother-in-law Surville and became the owner of six-eighths of

the company. He obtained the collaboration of the critic Gustave Planche, of Charles Bernard, a poet from Nodier's circle, of Alphonse Karr, and the young Théophile Gautier, whom he met at this time and who became his friend and biographer. But he himself contributed numerous texts to *La Chronique*: literary criticism signed under pseudonyms, political articles and three short marvels, *The Atheist's Mass*, *The Commission in Lunacy*, and *Facino Cane*, which, in due course, would become part of *The Human Comedy*. However, subscriptions – the only way of selling a review at that time – did not keep up, finances faltered, and in July 1836 the company was dissolved. Balzac's debts increased once more.

Four years later, however, he did a similar thing again, founding with the journalist Armand Dutacq the *Revue Parisienne*, whose first issue came out in July 1840, announcing a 128-page issue on the 25th of each month, to be sold for one franc.[19] Balzac himself wrote all the 396 pages contained in the three issues of the *Revue*. Among these texts, besides *Z. Marcas* in the first issue and *A Prince of Bohemia* in the second, the most celebrated was his review of *La Chartreuse de Parme*, seventy-two pages under the title *Études sur M. Beyle*.[20] Stendhal was no stranger to Balzac. He had met him in one or other of the salons they frequented – 'I had twice met M. Beyle in society in the course of twelve years, before I took the liberty of complimenting him on *La Chartreuse de Parme* when I encountered him on the Boulevard des Italiens' – and he noted in *The Firm of Nucingen* (1837), 'One of the most spiritual and profound men of our time, Stendhal.'[21] He had read *Le Rouge et le Noir* and one might see a reminder of Mathilde de la Mole's challenge – planning, if her father expelled Julien, to go out on his arm through the carriage

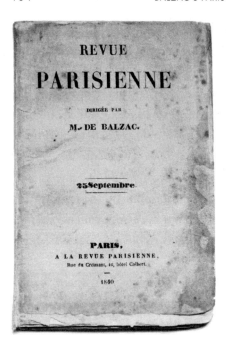

Cover of the *Revue Parisienne*,
25 September 1840 (Maison
de Balzac)

gate at high noon – in the scandal caused by Antoinette de
Langeais leaving her liveried coach in front of de Montriveau's
hôtel in broad daylight.[22]

La Chartreuse de Parme was published in March 1839. On 5
April, Balzac wrote to Stendhal: 'One should never delay pleas-
ing those who have given us pleasure. *La Chartreuse* is a great
and beautiful book. I tell you this without flattery, without envy,
for I would be incapable of writing it, and one can frankly praise
what is not of one's own trade. I make frescos and you have made
Italian statues.' But the letter contains 'not criticisms but obser-
vations', the strangest of which is the reproach for having clearly
set the action in Parma: 'You have made a huge mistake in specifying Parma, you should have named neither the state nor the
city, leaving it to the imagination to find the Prince of Modena,

his minister or anyone else.'[23] This is a curious criticism coming from the man who set his *Scenes of Provincial Life* in Saumur, Guérande, Limoges, Alençon, or Issoudun with such meticulous accuracy. But, a few months after this letter, in the very long article in the *Revue Parisienne*, Balzac found words worthy of the work:

M. Beyle has written a book in which the sublime bursts forth from one chapter to the next. He has produced, at an age when men rarely find great subjects, and after having written a score of extremely witty volumes, a work that can only be appreciated by truly superior souls and minds; finally, he has written the modern *Prince*, the novel that Machiavelli would have written, had he lived banished from Italy in the nineteenth century. The greatest obstacle to M. Beyle's deserved renown comes from the fact that *La Chartreuse de Parme* can only find readers capable of enjoying it among ministers, observers, the most distinguished people in society, the most distinguished artists, in short, among the twelve or fifteen hundred people who are at the head of Europe. Do not be surprised, then, that in the ten months since this surprising work was published, there is not a single journalist who has read it, understood it, or studied it, who has announced it, analysed it and praised it, or has even alluded to it. I myself, who think I have a little understanding, read it for the third time recently: I found the work even more beautiful, and I felt in my soul the kind of happiness that comes from doing a good deed.

This text, which today appears to be the praise of one great writer by another, was something quite different at the time. Balzac was at the height of his fame, while those who appreciated Stendhal were a happy few. The great critic of the time, Sainte-Beuve, had little regard for Beyle, to say the least: 'I have just reread, or tried to, Stendhal's novels; they are frankly detestable.' The same man, moreover, held Baudelaire to be 'a nice young fellow, fine in language and quite classical in form', and in Balzac he found a style 'so often ticklish and dissolving, enervated, roseate, and veined with all sorts of hues, of a delicious corruption, quite Asiatic as our masters used to say' – in other words, almost everything that Balzac's style is not.[24]

In the third issue of the *Revue Parisienne*, the prudent Dutacq noticed the deficit and decided to stop the adventure. Balzac had worked alone for three months and only increased his debts by several thousand francs. But no matter, his relationship with the press had changed and he would play a leading role in the great revolution in daily newspapers that took place in 1836.

On 1 August of that year, two new newspapers appeared simultaneously: *La Presse*, founded by Émile de Girardin; and *Le Siècle*, from Armand Dutacq.[25] These dailies were nothing like what had existed until then: large format like the London *Times*, a reduced price thanks to advertising (40 francs per year, or 2 cents per issue), and the presence on the front page of a feuilleton – an extract from a novel that would appear in its entirety in successive issues ('continued in the next issue'). To fill this section, Girardin reconciled himself with Balzac. The two men quarrelled many times in their lives – previously in 1834, when Balzac wrote to his sister: 'I have fallen out with Girardin and we will not see one another again.'[26] But this time Balzac's support was essential for the new journal. Girardin calls him 'My dear sulky', and makes amends: 'Our break-up has not for a moment destroyed in me the old affection that we have for each other . . . and if I was wrong about you, I would like nothing better than to put things right.'[27] Balzac agreed to try out the new formula with *The Old Maid*, an ironic and cruel 'scene from provincial life' which appeared over twelve issues in October–November 1836. It was the first novel to be published in serial form in a French daily newspaper, and thereafter almost all of Balzac's novels were to appear in instalments in one or other of the main newspapers before being published in book-shops in the form of octavo volumes. However, as Théophile Gautier notes, 'Balzac's feuilletons did not have the same success as those of Dumas or Sue, because he published his novels in periodicals and daily papers just as he wrote them, without building up suspense to trap the interest at the end of each feuil-leton, and make people want to know what was coming next.'[28] Balzac clearly had a different conception of his work from Dumas or Sue, and there was no question of his modifying his texts to adapt them to serial format.

The publication of Balzac's novels in newspapers was not without its problems. Girardin wrote to him in November 1836: 'We have received so many complaints about the choice of sub-ject and the freedom of certain descriptions that the manager of *La Presse* has asked the author of *The Old Maid* to choose a subject other than that of the courtesan Esther, the "Torpedo", a subject which, through the description it contains, is likely to be read by everyone, and raises opposition right from the start.'[29] And six months later: 'I would be obliged to remind you that *La Presse* is addressed to 15,000 subscribers, and in the salons it has most readers among women. So if the subject permits there to be nothing [in *La Femme supérieure*, which would become *The Lesser Bourgeoisie*] that offends their susceptibility to modesty, that will be a great chance for immense success.'[30]

To accusations of immorality, which today seem even stranger than for *Madame Bovary* or *Les Fleurs du mal*, Balzac replied in the preface to *La Femme supérieure*:

> Such and such a newspaper has asked for a piece that is neither too long nor too short, that can fit into so many columns and at such a price. The author goes to his store and says: I have *La Maison Nucingen*! It so happens that *La Maison Nucingen*, which is suitable for the length, the width and the price, talks about things that are too thorny to fit in with the newspaper's policy. *La Maison Nucingen* remains on the author's hands. Well, take *La Torpille* [the Torpedo]! La Torpille is a *grisette*, and we have already announced *La Vieille Fille* [*The Old Maid*]. Our readers, who read the horrors of the *Gazette des Tribunaux* and the infamies of the advertisements, have howled because of the overly large breasts of Mademoiselle Cormon [the heroine of *La Vieille Fille*] and the comical fraud of a Norman *grisette* [in *Béatrix*] who claims to be pregnant in order to get pious souls and an old libertine to give her the sum needed for a little trip to Paris. Give us something between sermon and literature, something that makes columns and no scandal, that is dramatic without danger, comical without comedy; guillotine a man, do not depict either an impotent shopkeeper or a too bold banker, they do not exist.

And in the original preface to *Père Goriot*, Balzac makes an 'examination of conscience', a witty picture where, in two columns, he counts the erudite women and the criminal women in his work, showing that he is wrongly accused because the former are more numerous than the latter. This did not prevent his work from being blacklisted by the Vatican.

Immorality was not the only theme singled out by those who criticized Balzac in the press. We may be surprised today by the violence of writings against 'this prodigious meteor who will cover our country with a cloud of glory, like a strange and exceptional sunrise, a polar aurora inundating the icy desert with its fairy lights', as Baudelaire would write one day.[31] Thus, on *A Great Man of the Provinces in Paris* (the second part of *Lost Illusions*), *Le Corsaire, journal des spectacles, de la littérature et des arts* had this to say: 'This book, into which one can enter only as into a sewer, this book full of fetid descriptions, this disgusting and cynical book, is quite simply Balzac's revenge against the press'; and under the pen of Jules Janin: 'At no time of his talent has M. Balzac's thought been more diffuse, his invention more languid, or his style more incorrect.' On *The Peasants*, a certain Alexandre Thomas wrote in the *Revue de Paris*: 'It is an impotent hatred of our morals and our ideals, it is a poor insult that they are trying to throw cavalierly in the face of French democracy . . . And all this, in what a fashion, by God! With the exquisite taste of those ill-mannered parvenus who complain incessantly about their readers because they have only just won them.'[32] Such offensive language is not to be found in reviews of the novels of Victor Hugo, Eugène Sue, or Alexandre Dumas, because Balzac's dissection of the society of his time was unparalleled, unacceptable, and unforgivable. And the character himself was so alien to the norms of the time, from the way he dressed to his public rantings, that he attracted the hatred of all those for whom a writer worthy of the name must be a member of the beau monde and not 'an ill-mannered parvenu'. It was undoubtedly for this reason that he would not be elected to the Académie, which preferred the Duc de Noailles. Balzac received four votes, including those of Hugo and Lamartine.

'M. de Noailles is considered a bourgeois and I have debts, *palsambleu!*'[33]

This hostility – not to mention the often-virulent criticism of his plays – no doubt explains why Balzac described the press of his time as riddled with cynicism, sold to the highest bidder, devoid of culture and convictions. In 'De L'État actuel de la littérature', an article published in the old Legitimist newspaper *La Quotidienne*, he wrote:

> The evil produced by journalism is much greater; it kills, it devours real talent. Newspapers, with the exception of two or three purely literary sheets in which only conscientious works appear, newspapers are another Society of Jesus, taking away from the country its best minds and engaging them to waste in often admirably written columns the richest hopes of literature.[34]

Later, in *La Monographie de la presse parisienne*: 'The Press, like woman, is admirable and sublime when it offers a lie, it does not let you go until it has forced you to believe it, and it deploys the greatest qualities in this struggle – in which the public, as stupid as a husband, always succumbs.'[35] But it is, above all, in his novels, in *A Daughter of Eve* and especially *Lost Illusions*, that Balzac settles accounts with journalism. Lucien de Rubempré, penniless, freezes with his friends of the Cénacle in a garret on Rue des Quatre-Vents. 'On several occasions he talked of plunging into journalism, but his friends always said: "For Heaven's sake don't." "That would be the end of the fine, gentle Lucien we love and know," said d'Arthez.' And Fulgence Ridal:

> You only too obviously possess the qualities of a journalist: brilliance and versatility of thought. You would never deny

yourself a shaft of wit, even if it reduced a friend to tears. I see
journalists in the theatre foyer, and they horrify me. Journalism is an inferno, a bottomless pit of iniquity, falsehood and
treachery: one can only pass through it and emerge from it
unsullied if one is shielded as Dante was by the divine laurels
of Virgil.[36]

The weak Lucien would not heed this advice, nor would he listen
to Lousteau, a disillusioned journalist: 'Newspaper-proprietors
are contractors; we're their masons . . . I feel sorry for you. I see
in you what I used to be, and I'm sure that in a year or two you'll
be as I am now.'[37] Lucien becomes a journalist, he is successful,
and he betrays his friends, 'the grave and serious men of the
Cénacle'; he goes from liberal-Voltairian to royalist-romantic,
and ends up disgraced and ruined. The world of the press is
pitiless.

Some among the journalists in *The Human Comedy*, however,
escape this damning judgement on the profession. There is the
melancholic Lousteau, driven from literature to journalism by
hunger; Blondet, 'a newspaper editor, a man of great spirit, but
disjointed, brilliant, capable, lazy, knowing himself to be
exploited, letting himself be exploited, perfidious as he is good,
by caprice; one of those men whom one loves and does not
esteem'; and Bixiou, writer and caricaturist (his model was
Henri Monnier), 'a misanthropic buffoon, acknowledged
supreme, by reason of his energetic and caustic wit; a very fiend
let loose now that he saw how he had squandered his intellect
in pure waste'.[38] These young men could be said to be support-
ing characters, but as a number of them appear in the *Scenes
from Parisian Life* (and elsewhere), they are in the end like
narrative pillars – gifted and superficial, witty, sometimes

The Cénacle (Nanteuil, Édition Furne)

mean, but capable of being generous, though often penniless. Their political and literary views vary according to the newspaper they work for. They are to be found at all the dinners of the pretty actresses, at Florine's and Coralie's, but also at Nucingen's and Madame d'Espard's, and their wit sparkles like champagne. One wonders whether Balzac does not sometimes envy the existence of his creatures, these men 'whom we love and do not esteem': their laziness, their carelessness, the freedom of their life so different from his own, engulfed in debts and hard work.

Publishers

In the testimonies of his friends and relatives, Balzac appears as a witty guest, a devoted friend, an attentive if not faithful lover – in short, a character full of charm beneath his unusual exterior. There is, however, one black mark: his conduct towards his publishers. It is certainly hard in retrospect to pity them: weren't they lucky to have such a glorious author? Isn't it partly thanks to him that their names have come down to us? Yes, but the fact remains that they had to endure his endless delays, his bad faith, his financial demands – and if a relationship generally began in trust and sometimes friendship, it almost always ended in acrimonious exchanges, letters of rupture, even lawsuits.

The reasons for this lie primarily in his way of working. Balzac treated a first set of proofs as a mere draft, covering them with corrections if he did not rewrite the entire text in the margins in the form of hard-to-decipher scribbles (one of his common points with Proust). And, since he was an extreme perfectionist, he needed a second, then third set of proofs – and woe betide the printer or editor who failed to provide these. From

Angoulême, he wrote to his mother: 'I have received today the packet of proofs; but please explain to Gosselin that I need the whole typesetting, the whole work before my eyes . . . If I correct one galley at a time, I will lose two weeks on this work, while if I have everything in front of me and correct it all at

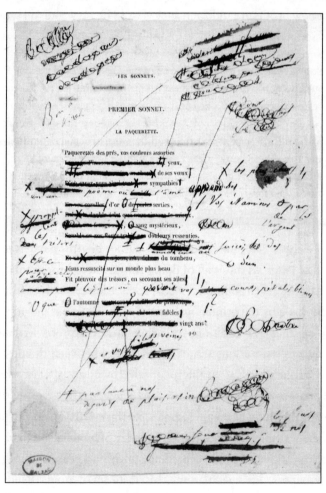

Proof page of *Illusions perdues* (Maison de Balzac)

once, I will only need three days.'[1] A fortnight later, he wrote to Gosselin: 'On the 15th [August] you will have my corrected galleys,' before changing his mind: 'I thought it was Friday and it is Saturday; when I work through the nights, I easily forget the days; I beg you, take back the corrections from the printers and typeset them again, it will cost less. You will see from the galleys that new proofs are indispensable.'[2] In 1840, he wrote to Hyppolite Souverain:

> You have sent me the right sheet 3 of the *Curé* [*de Tours*] volume II, but I do not have the right sheet 2. It is impossible for me to read, or give the go-ahead, or to deal with the galleys you sent me, without the old corrected proofs – it is boring to repeat the same things. At 1st sight, I see the divisions and the titles of chapters omitted – and I *no longer* know what I am doing, so I wait. I have kept 20 sheets of the first galleys, as I don't know what copy is needed; I have asked for it to be set to page, to know how it comes out, before I give the go-ahead to print.[3]

It is easy to imagine a publisher's face when they receive this kind of letter, as this way of doing things led to exorbitant additional costs: each additional set of proofs, each cycle of corrections to be made by the printer, was very expensive and at the publisher's expense.[4] In addition, the proliferation of proof sets led to delays, as the various stages had to travel between the printers and Balzac's lodging at the time, which was not always easy to ascertain.

But the main cause of disputes between Balzac and his publishers was money. Since the bankruptcy of his print shop on Rue des Marais in 1828, his debts had steadily increased – with his newspapers, his speculations, his taste for luxury, the works done on his successive residences. Money slipped through his fingers and his attempts to rectify the situation were always a disaster. He constantly had to find enough to live on, and escape – sometimes narrowly – the debtors' prison on Rue de Clichy. His only source of income was the sale of his work to periodicals and the 'book trade', that is, publishers. As we have seen, these publishers had been in crisis since the end of the Restoration: they paid little and were slow to do so. Royalties were around one franc per copy and rarely were more than one or two thousand copies of a new novel printed.[5] Hugo's novels had print runs of two thousand copies, and *The Chouans*, Balzac's first book, one thousand.[6]

What is more, the royalties fixed on signing of the 'treaty' (we would say 'contract') were paid by promissory notes with an often-distant maturity. Thus, the contract with the faithful Canel and Levavasseur for *The Physiology of Marriage* foresaw a print run of 1,500 copies and indicated that 'the sum of fifteen hundred francs is payable in their bills at one year's date'.[7] That left plenty of time for the publisher to go bankrupt, in which case the bill would be worthless. The author could certainly negotiate (discount) the bill before its due date by seeking out a Gobseck or a Gigonnet – but, if they accepted the bill, it would be under conditions that were all the more unfavourable given the publisher's serious financial difficulties. There are many examples of such disastrous transactions in *The Human Comedy*.

So much so that, in order to stay afloat, Balzac had constantly to supply an enormous amount of material. It is to this constraint that we owe the immensity of *The Human Comedy*: twelve volumes in the Pléiade edition, twenty-six volumes in his own 1845 catalogue, which foresaw 137 volumes 'of which 50 remain to be done'.[8] But fifteen hours of work through day and night were not enough; Balzac ended up signing contracts for novels that he said were finished when they had been barely sketched out or not even begun at all.

From Aix-les-Bains, where he followed the Duchesse de Castries in the autumn of 1832, he wrote to his mother:

> I worked for three days and three nights, I wrote a volume in-18° titled *The Country Doctor*. A traveller is taking it to Mame; as it is only 200 pages in-18°, he can have it all typeset, and I can sign it off for printing before I leave for Italy, which will not be until 10 October. He will let me have 500 francs in Rome and 500 francs in Naples. He will have my instructions.[9]

A week later, in a letter to Mame: 'My mother will receive from me, if she has not already done so, A COMPLETE MANU-SCRIPT! . . . titled *The Country Doctor*, which is intended for you. Pay close attention, Master Mame.' It was

> a book which the concierge and the great lady can both read. I have taken the Gospel and the Catechism as models, two books that flow exceptionally well, and made this my own . . . Now *I want one franc per copy, and will let you print 1,300 for a thousand*; price it as low as you can; why I want a thousand francs is because I am leaving for Italy and I want to afford my trip.[10]

And he gives Mame all sorts of details about proof and press dates – all without having written a line of the book.[11] From Geneva, in October, he sends him a reassuring letter: 'My dear Master Mame, or Father Mame if you like it better, I thank you first of all for your kind and affectionate letter . . . Nothing has changed with *The Country Doctor* and I can confide in you, who will understand the importance of such a secret, that I am returning to France for three months, for several reasons, the least of which is this: I have *The Doctor* to be printed.'[12]

And further on, in the same letter:

> Now, let's talk about *The Doctor* – It is done – But I need to guard
> myself today against my own facility, even though it is the fruit of
> my studies and my work. So I want to review it and above all, to
> examine it with my excellent adviser. Then I thought that two
> weeks more or less would not be too much for a work of this
> nature.[13]

In November, he invites Mame to Nemours, as 'we will be
better off this way and you will gain something, *a fine and
good manuscript*'.[14] In fact, Mame left with only summaries of
the chapters. That was too much: in June 1833, Mame sued
Balzac before the court of first instance of the Seine for non-
performance of the contract, demanding 3,000 francs in
damages and 50 francs per day interest for the delay in deliver-
ing the manuscript.[15] At the hearing, Balzac presented himself
with the proofs of *The Country Doctor* – which he had finished
and had typeset at his own expense – and claimed the right to
publish it with the publisher of his choice. The court refused
and kept the right to publish the book with Mame. Balzac was
furious and went to the printer's the next day, had the door
opened, and jumbled the typesetting to make it unusable. But
in the end, following an arbitration ruling, *The Country Doctor*
was published by 'that despicable executioner who bears the
name of Mame, who has blood and bankruptcies on his face,
and can add to the tears of those he has ruined the sorrows of a
poor and hard-working man'.[16]

Such travails are not the exception in Balzac's relations with
his publishers. Barely out of prison (the 'Hôtel des Haricots',
where men who had not fulfilled their obligations as national
guards were locked up), he wrote to Madame Hanska:

Oh, now, enough is enough. Do you know what I am being inter-
rupted by? By a legal document from Madame Béchet, who is
summoning me to provide her with two octavo volumes within
twenty-four hours, and demanding fifty francs for each day of
delay! I must be a great criminal, and God must want me to atone
for my crimes! Never has there been such a torment. This woman
has had ten octavo volumes from me in two years! She complains
that she has not had twelve![17]

Balzac's procrastination and delays were not insignifcant in the
financial difficulties of two publishers who had bet everything
on him, Urbain Canel and Edmond Werdet – whose bankruptcy
in 1837 was directly linked to the numerous notes he had issued
to meet Balzac's demands for money.

It was also the successive delays in the delivery of *The Wild
Ass's Skin* that caused Balzac's falling out with Charles Gosselin,
one of the greatest Romantic publishers who counted Hugo,
Béranger, Casimir Delavigne, Vigny, Lamartine, and George
Sand among his authors. He offered Balzac to be his sole publisher: 'I will buy all your books, do not look for other booksellers,
it seems to me that this is not something to be said to everyone
when you are a publisher well placed enough to have more pro-
posals from reputed authors than it is possible to accommodate.'[18]
Balzac did not accept this offer. He did not want to be 'like a
tethered dog', and sometimes gives the impression of deriving
pleasure from his superb aplomb (*The Country Doctor*: 'It's done!'),
and from his way of getting out of the most tricky situations:
manners that were famous enough, sufficiently constitutive of
his public persona, for Baudelaire to mock him nicely with
'Comment on paie ses dettes quand on a du génie'.[19] In the end,
the character in *The Human Comedy* that Balzac reminds us of is
Vautrin, the man of the most improbable expedients, the most

unexpected rebounds. Was this not the kind of 'incarnation' that the former inmate of the Collège de Vendôme dreamt of when he aspired to the National Assembly and membership of the Académie, never losing the hope of one day being rich. Baudelaire again was not wrong in assimilating the novelist and his characters in his famous address at the end of 'The Salon of 1846':

> For the heroes of the Iliad are but pigmies compared to you, Vautrin, Rastignac and Birotteau! – and you, Fontanarès, who dared not publicly declaim your sorrows in the funereal and tortured frock-coat which we all wear today! – and you, Honoré de Balzac, you the most heroic, the most extraordinary, the most romantic and the most poetic of all the characters that you have produced from your womb![20]

The great publishers of the Romantic period were not 'intellectuals' from the university: they were former booksellers – Gosselin, Levavasseur, Werdet, Renduel – or came from the printing industry, such as Buloz, a former proofreader, or Fournier, Mérimée's publisher, who started out with the Firmin-Didot print works. Among the publishers, however, there were some that never upset Balzac, such as Hippolyte Souverain, with whom his relations were always cordial and who often helped him during his stays abroad.[21] Another fruitful and peaceable contact was that of Gervais Charpentier, a former clerk of Ladvocat. Of Charpentier, it can be said that he was the saviour of the French book trade, which was seriously threatened by Belgian counterfeiting: in 1838, he launched the Bibliothèque Charpentier, composed of small books in sextodecimo format, whose compact layout made it possible to fit the equivalent of two octavo volumes into a single volume.[22] These ancestors of the paperback, printed in tens of thousands of copies, were sold for 3.50 francs instead of the usual 15 francs for books in reading-room format. Three years after its launch, the Bibliothèque Charpentier had nearly 200 volumes in print – titles certainly published already in 'normal' editions, as with today's paperback imprints. In 1838, Balzac signed a contract with Charpentier giving him the right to print 36,500 copies of his works, to be chosen from a list that included *Old Man Goriot*, *The Country Doctor*, *The Wild Ass's Skin*, *The Lily in the Valley*, and *César Birotteau* – in print runs that were out of all proportion to those of traditional publishing.

October 1841 marked a major turning point in Balzac's publishing career: he signed with 'Messrs Furne, publisher at 55 Rue Saint-André-des-Arts, Hetzel and Paulin, of 33 Rue de Seine, and J. J. Dubouchet, at the same street and number, jointly and severally' – a contract which granted them 'the exclusive right to print and sell his complete works, under the general title of *The Human Comedy*'. This right included 'not only the works published to date, but also those that will appear and be published during the course of the present contract'.[23] Balzac was to receive fifty centimes per volume of at least twenty-four leaves (one leaf was sixteen pages), with an advance of 15,000 francs in promissory notes.

Thus was born the Furne imprint, which could, in fact, have been named after Hetzel, the real project manager of the enterprise. This edition is still a reference today, and it is thanks to it that we have texts finalized by Balzac himself, selected by him, classified in the order he indicated and reworked at length, as he explained to Madame Hanska:

> *The Human Comedy* takes me 200 hours a month, as I read each
> proof twice, and I corrected the edition that serves as a manuscript,
> which makes three times, and at three hours per sheet, there are
> thirty per volume, judge this work of which I will never speak to
> you. It is overwhelming, because it is a question of finding my
> mistakes and correcting them.[24]

Balzac was also busy commissioning woodcuts to represent
his characters among the main illustrators of the time. He wrote
to Hetzel: 'In the first volume of *Scenes of Provincial Life*, we
must give Abbé Troubert and Pierrette to Gérard-Seguin, Abbé
Birotteau to Meissonier, Philippe Bridau, Colonel Gouraud and
the lawyer Vinet to Monnier; Mother Lorrain to Meissonier – the
Black Sheep to Gavarni and Roguin to Daumier.'[25]

For this great affair, Balzac wanted a foreword. Nodier and
then George Sand withdrew, and finally Hetzel convinced him
to write what was to become the famous *Avant-propos*:

> Let's get to work, then, fat old man; allow a thin editor to speak to
> your fatness in this way. You know it's for a good purpose. It's a
> matter of an advertisement. If I knew how to write, I would do so,
> but in advertising a merchant is better than a poet. How should we
> publish your books, which would appear for the first time under
> this overall title, *La Comédie humaine*, with the first line as follows:
> 'I give this name (*La Comédie humaine*) to my complete works for
> the following reasons, etc. etc.'[26]

The tone of this letter shows the friendship between Balzac and
Hetzel, and as the correspondence progresses, we hope to see
this exceptional relationship last. Unfortunately, promissory
notes written by Balzac to Hetzel and passed by the latter to an
inconvenient creditor led to their falling out in 1846 – and this

Vautrin (Daumier, Édition Furnet)

time Balzac was not necessarily to blame. But, in the end, it does not matter, the Furne/Hetzel edition would be a glorious conclusion to Balzac's adventures with his publishers.

At the Theatre

In Balzac, as a man of the theatre, one can obviously find traits in common with the man who was writing *The Human Comedy* at the same time: the relentlessness of his work, the proliferation of projects, the art and manner of keeping people waiting – theatre impresarios, perhaps still more anxious than publishers. But, in changing his activity, Balzac also changed his method, and radically so. The novelist capable of suing for unread proofs, complaining to the printers about minute details, rewriting his works at each reprint – this perfectionist disappears as soon as Balzac writes for the theatre. For him, this was an activity designed to earn money. In the words of Théophile Gautier:

> The theatre, as we know, brings in much more money than books; the continuity of performances, with a fairly high level of royalties, quickly produces considerable sums. Balzac, who meditated, elaborated and corrected his novels with such dogged meticulousness, seemed, when it came to the theatre, to be caught by the vertigo of speed. Not only did he not rewrite his plays eight or ten times as

he did his stories, he did not even do so at all. As soon as he had the first idea, he would set a day for reading it and call his friends to listen.

Gautier relates how he and his friends were urgently summoned to Buisson's house one evening:

> 'Hurry up, you should have been here an hour ago. Tomorrow I am reading a great drama in five acts to Harel.' 'And you want our opinion,' we replied, settling into armchairs like people preparing for a long reading. From our attitude, Balzac guessed our thoughts and said to us with the simplest air: 'The drama is not finished.' 'Well,' I said, 'we'll have to postpone the reading for six weeks.' 'No, we're going to dash off the *dramorama* to get the cash. At a time as this I have a very busy deadline.' And he divided the acts among his friends present. 'Tell me the subject, tell me the plan, draw the characters in a few words,' I replied, somewhat aghast. 'Ah!' he exclaimed with an air of superb despondency and magnificent disdain, 'if I have to tell you the subject, we'll never be finished!'[1]

('Dash off the *dramorama* to get the cash': an example of the vulgarity which, as we have seen, so displeased Proust's mother).

Père Goriot was published by Werdet in March 1835. In April of the same year, two theatres, the Vaudeville and the Variétés, announced a *Père Goriot*, and the two versions, works by two different authors, were performed simultaneously. In the following years, *Le Gars* (based on *The Chouans*) was performed at the Ambigu-Comique, *Le Rêve d'un savant* (Balthazar Claes from *The Quest of the Absolute*) at the Gymnase-Dramatique, *César Birotteau* at the Théâtre du Panthéon, Madame Marneffe (based on *Cousin Bette*) also at the Gymnase, and even, in 1839, *Les Treizes* at the Opéra-Comique, with lyrics by Scribe,

music by Halévy, and the heroes as young Neapolitan govern-
ors in the land of Fra Diavolo. All these plays have little to
do with Balzac's novels; they tend towards vaudeville with
happy endings instead of the dark denouements of *The Human
Comedy*.[2]

Why did Balzac lend himself to such caricatures of his work?
Quite simply, he got a third of the royalties. From Poland he
wrote to his mother:

> Don't forget to go to the theatre agent, who lives on Rue Saint-
> Marc, 4 or 6, on the second floor, M. Hostein will tell you the
> name, and there you will receive what I can get back from my 1/3
> in *Madame Marneffe* and a remainder of the account of *La
> Marâtre* . . . and from then on he will pay you my royalties every
> 8th or 9th of each month.[3]

Balzac favoured the proliferation of plays bearing the names of
his novels, and he even imagined buffoonish subjects capable
of enriching this repertoire. In 1844 he wrote to Madame
Hanska: 'Next year, I will earn 100,000 francs with my pen, and
we shall see!'

How were these para-Balzacian works distributed in the theatrical landscape of the 1840s? They were not performed on
the main stages – the Théâtre-Français, the Odéon, the Opéra,
the Italiens – which are often mentioned in *The Human Comedy*
and where Balzac had some of his 'real' plays performed. At the
other end of the spectrum, they did not go to the little theatres
of the 'Boulevard du Crime' (an expression that Balzac, as we
have seen, does not use), where melodramas were performed and
tickets cost one franc against five or six at the Théâtre-Français.[4]
The venues for these plays were located between the two, on that

long stretch of boulevard between Rue Montmartre and the section of Boulevard du Temple destroyed when Place du Château-d'Eau (now de la République) was built.

These buffooneries were performed, among others, at the Variétés, whose portico still exists, facing the entrance to the Passage des Panoramas; at the Ambigu-Comique, a magnificent hall from the eighteenth century on the corner of Boulevard Saint-Martin and Rue de Bondy (now René-Boulanger), destroyed with Malraux's approval in the 1960s; at the Théâtre de la Porte-Saint-Martin; at the Gymnase-Dramatique, on Boulevard de Bonne-Nouvelle; and also at the Théâtre du Vaudeville, the Théâtre-Historique, and the Panorama-Dramatique . . . as if Balzac dreamed of occupying all the Paris theatres with titles borrowed from *The Human Comedy*. What is certain is that he was planning a novel entitled *Le Théâtre tel qu'il est*, 'a work similar to that which I have done on journalism, and intended to make known the backstage world, the awful, hideous, comic, terrible drama that precedes the rise of the curtain.'[5]

Balzac did not complete this project, but theatre and opera are omnipresent in his Parisian novels. They are often a place of amorous encounter: at the start of *The Secrets of the Princesse de Cadignan*, the princess whose misfortunes had not altered her beauty ('the only thing she saved of her departed opulence', that is, from the time when she had been Duchesse de Maufrigneuse) tells her friend, the Marquise d'Espard: 'Every Friday, at the Opéra, I observed a young man, about thirty years of age, in the orchestra stalls, who evidently came there for me. He was always in the same stall, gazing at me with eyes of fire, but, seemingly, saddened by the distance between us, perhaps by the hopelessness of reaching me.'[6] In *Old Man Goriot*, the decisive meeting of Rastignac with Delphine de Nucingen takes place 'at the fashionable theatre' (the Italiens).[7] 'Delphine de Nucingen was more than a little flattered to be the sole object of the attentions of Madame de Beauséant's young, handsome, elegant cousin; he had eyes only for her.'[8] The scene is sometimes more tense: when Lucien de Rubempré is humiliated at the Opéra, guessing 'that he looked like a man who had dressed for the first time in his life'; or in the unforgettable opening of *A Harlot High and Low*, at the masked ball at the Opéra, when 'Bixiou called out: "Esther?" The unfortunate creature turned quickly on hearing her name, saw the malicious individual, and lowered

Père Goriot
(Daumier, Édition
Furne)

her head like a dying person who has just yielded up her last breath.'[9]

But in *The Human Comedy* the theatre is not only a social place, it is also a place of work. Balzac describes at length the life of the beautiful Florine,

> that treadmill life, in which the actress is forced to rehearsals under pain of fines, to the reading of new pieces, to the constant study of new roles, at a time when two or three hundred plays are performed each year in Paris. At each representation, Florine changes her dress two or three times; often she comes home exhausted and half-dead; but before she can rest, she must wash off with various cosmetics the white and the red she has applied, and clean all the powder from her hair, if she has played a part from the eighteenth century. She scarcely has time for food. When she plays, an actress can live no life of her own; she can neither dress, nor eat, nor talk. Florine often has no time to sup. On returning from a play, which lasts, in these days, till after midnight, she still has her night toilet to do, and orders to give, not going to bed before two in the morning. She must rise early enough to study her part, order her dresses, try them on, breakfast, read her love-letters, answer them, discuss with the leader of the 'claque' the place for her plaudits, pay for the triumphs of the last month in solid cash, and bespeak those of the month ahead.[10]

It was at the Panorama-Dramatique that Lucien de Rubempré met Florine and Coralie:

> The Panorama-Dramatique, now replaced by a private house, was a charming theatre standing opposite Rue Charlot in the Boulevard du Temple. Two of its managing bodies in turn succumbed without scoring a single success, although Vignol, one of the actors who took over from Potier, made his *début* there, as well as Florine, the actress who was to become so famous five years later.[11]

Guided by Lousteau, Lucien is introduced to the world of the backstage:

> Then, walking up a few damp steps, the provincial poet arrived behind the scenes, where the strangest of spectacles awaited him. The narrowness of the supporting struts, the height of the theatre, the ladders with their lamps, the flats, so ugly when seen from close quarters, the actors' heavy make-up, their costumes, so bizarre and made of such coarse material, the stagehands with their greasy jackets, the dangling ropes, the stage-manager striding around with his hat on, the extras sitting round, the hanging back-cloths, the firemen, all this array of dirty, hideous and tawdry objects was so unlike what Lucien had seen from out front that his astonishment was unbounded.[12]

Balzac's cruelty towards the theatre world was designed to show that the success or failure of a play depends above all on the claque and the journalists:

> As Lucien went out [from visiting Braulard, the head of the '*claqueurs*'], he saw filing in front of him the evil-smelling squad of *claqueurs* and ticket-touts, all wearing caps, well-worn trousers, threadbare frockcoats, with hangdog, dirty blue, dirty green, muddy, scraggy faces, long beards, with eyes that were at once ferocious and fawning, a nauseous population which lives and swarms in the Paris boulevards, sells safety-chains and 'gold' jewellery for twenty-five sous in the mornings, and in the evenings claps its hands under the theatre chandeliers; which in short adapts itself to all the unclean exigencies of Parisian life.[13]

And Lucien ensures Coralie's triumph in *The Alcade in Difficulties* with his first article, just as Lousteau will have Florine attacked 'in six newspapers' to extort money from the druggist Matifat, her protector. One might think that the description of a cynical and venal world, where blackmail and extortion are very close to the limelight, is a way for Balzac to take revenge for his setbacks in the theatre; but *Lost Illusions* was written at the end of the 1830s, whereas Balzac's plays date only from the 1840s.

The list of theatrical projects that Balzac toyed with, sketched out, and promised in those years is endless: *Prudhomme en bonne fortune*, in which he hoped for the collaboration of Henri Monnier; *L'Espion*; *Richard Coeur-d'éponge*; *Les Traînards de l'armée française*, a play that was 'for the time of Napoleon what Don Quixote is to chivalry'; *L'Éducation du Prince*; *Pierre et Catherine*, 'a great work in the style of Shakespeare'; *Le Vagabonde*; *Les Philanthropes*; and *Le Roi des mendiants*.[14] But he nevertheless completed and had performed five plays, two of which, while being resounding failures, nevertheless left their mark on their time: *Vautrin* and *Les Ressources de Quinola*.[15]

We have seen Balzac announcing to his stunned friends that *Vautrin* had not been written. He set to work on it, cloistering himself in Buisson's house. After several revisions to comply with the demands of the censors and the requests of Harel, the director of the Porte-Saint-Martin, rehearsals began in January 1840 with the illustrious Frédérick Lemaître in the title role. Balzac asked Gavarni for indications for Frédérick's costume: 'Yes, P'osper, we need the exact costume of a Mexican general from the time of the War of Independence.'[16] But despite all these efforts, the dark and mysterious Vautrin, whose disquieting presence haunts *Old Man Goriot*, *Lost Illusions*, and perhaps still more so *A Harlot High and Low*, has vanished into thin air when he enters the skin of the theatrical Vautrin. The plot is muddled, the dialogues interminable, the situations conventional, and even the names, always so accurate in *The Human Comedy*, do not sound right: the great female roles are the Duchesse de

Frédérick Lemaître (frontispiece of Eugène Mirecourt's book *Frédérick Lemaître*, 1858)

Montsorel and the Duchesse de Christoval – Balzac would never have allowed such mistakes in a novel.

Moreover, Balzac, always short of money, engaged in dubious speculation. Gozlan recounts:

> Guessing with what rare avidity the seats would be sought by all those whose minds he had charmed with his books for so many years, he saw a speculation both lucrative and permissible in the advance sale of tickets, a sale he undertook in agreement with the director of the Porte-Saint-Martin, who was only too happy with this unusual initiative. Not only did the placement of the tickets become certain, but it seemed to ensure as many friends and devoted supporters as spectators.

But between the sale of the tickets and the first performance, a much longer period of time elapsed than expected, during which

> seductions of all kinds took two-thirds of the seats out of the hands of the first purchasers and passed them on to a crowd of people unknown to or hostile to Balzac. So it happened that the lights, instead of showing a regular hall of friends, only lit up a noisy, unruly, mocking crowd, with neither the calm of a chosen society nor the frankness of the true public who buy their rights at the door.

The first three acts are boring, the actors mediocre, and the dialogue sluggish. The explosion occurs in Act IV, Scene II, when the Duchesse de Christoval says to her maid: 'General Crustamente, secret envoy of His Majesty Don Augustin I, Emperor of Mexico, what does that mean? Bring him in.' The appearance of Frédérick Lemaître – in a sky-blue suit, white trousers and a hat topped by a bird of paradise, a large sabre, a coppery complexion, a greasy accent, and above all a hairstyle reminiscent of Louis Philippe's quiff – triggered a veritable shambles. Gozlan:

> The hall no longer had dignity, calm, respect or behaviour; each box was the mouth of a great volcano whose crater was the parterre; a volcano of mockery, jeers, blasphemies, insults, and also threats; for here and there were a few good friends who remained faithful amidst this unheard-of anger, this unleashed rage.[17]

In short, it was a disaster. The next day's press was full of scorn, and the *Moniteur Parisien* of 15 October published an article stating that 'the immorality of the subject, despite having been mitigated by major deletions, was aggravated by the main actor. The minister of the interior has pronounced the banning of the work.' Despite the representations of Victor Hugo, well known at court, and Alexandre Dumas, a favourite of the public, the minister (Charles de Rémusat) maintained the ban, writing in his *Mémoires*: 'To have defied the theatrical press and displeased Harel, Hugo and Balzac did me the greatest good, and honest people felt that they had not been abandoned.'[18]

Balzac was not to be discouraged. In September 1841, he wrote to Madame Hanska that 'in order to be able to pay my debts more surely, I will finish a comedy for the month of December, entitled *Les Rubriques de Quinola*'.[19] And in December, he signed a contract with the Odéon theatre, the first article of which states that 'M. de Balzac obliges himself to read in fifteen days from today to MM. the Director and Actors a comedy in five acts with a prologue entitled *Les Ressources de*

Quinola'.[20] Gozlan recounts the reading in the foyer of the
Odéon:

> Heavy at first, pasty and awkward, Balzac's voice became clearer
> as he progressed in the reading; later it acquired a serious, perfect,
> velvety tone, and finally, when it was launched and the passion
> followed the drama, it obeyed the most delicate intentions of the
> phrase, the most fleeting undulations of the dialogue . . . But
> suddenly the joy, the pleasure, the gaiety, the happiness stopped
> dead, like a carriage whose wheel has broken. What was happen-
> ing? It seemed that, at the end of the fourth act, after blowing his
> nose, wiping his forehead and face, searching under his ample
> white waistcoat for his braces to pull up his trousers, which had
> slipped several notches by the violent exercise he had undergone,
> Balzac announced to his audience, throbbing with anxiety, that the
> fifth act was not written.[21]

Nevertheless, the play was accepted, and rehearsals began in
January 1842.

The action takes place in Spain during the reign of Philip II.
The news of the defeat of the Invincible Armada has just been
received. Fontanarès, an unknown inventor, has developed a
boat powered by a steam engine in spite of the Inquisition, with
the help of Quinola, a Sganarelle-like character whose practical-
ity (*ressources*) compensates for the hero's dreamy nature. But in
the fifth act, jealousy finally frustrates Fontanarès's invention
and the boat catches fire in the port of Barcelona. The play was
much better than *Vautrin* and could have been a success if Balzac
had not once again made mistakes with the launch. He refused
to give tickets to journalists, naturally earning their dislike. He
convinced the director of the Odéon to let him sell the tickets
himself at exorbitant prices. He refused to use touts but himself

demanded an extravagant hundred tickets. Finally, on the evening of the premiere, 19 March, the hall was half empty; whistles and bird calls drowned out the voices of the actors. It was a new disaster.

'Quinola,' Balzac wrote to Madame Hanska, 'was the object of a memorable battle, similar to that of Hernani. People came to whistle throughout the play; from one end to the other, with no desire to hear it.'[22]

By a cruel irony of history, *Mercadet* (*Le Faiseur*), Balzac's best play and a remote adaptation of *César Birotteau*, was never performed in his lifetime. It was produced successfully at the Gymnase-Dramatique on 23 August 1851, and went through fifty-six performances. The Comédie Française revived it in 1993 in a production by Jean-Paul Roussillon, with Michel Aumont in the title role and Catherine Hiegel in that of the main female character, the beautiful Virginie.

Friends, Politics, and the Realism of Balzac's Paris

How did the former boarder at the Collège de Vendôme, son of a family with neither title nor wealth, enter the Parisian world that was so brilliant in his day? How did he become one of its leading characters while remaining himself a sort of ill-mannered parvenu?

Before he began *The Human Comedy*, at the 'turning point of 1830', Balzac's initiation into Paris society was owed mainly to two women, the Duchesse d'Abrantès and the Marquise (later Duchesse) de Castries. Laure d'Abrantès had known glorious hours under the Empire when she had married General Junot, a comrade-in-arms of Napoleon who had made him Duc d'Abrantès. She had had an eventful love life, including an affair with Metternich, then Austrian ambassador in Paris. But Junot went mad and committed suicide in 1813, and from then on fortune would abandon the duchess, who was still beautiful but impoverished when Balzac met her in 1825. During their romance, she introduced him to Madame Récamier, who received

the most prominent writers and artists, from Lamartine to Toc-
queville, François Gérard to Antonio Canova, in the company
of Chateaubriand at the Abbaye-aux-Bois.[1] Laure also accompanied Balzac to Rue d'Anjou in the Faubourg Saint-Honoré, the
home of Princesse Bagration, who had a salon frequented by
Benjamin Constant, Stendhal, the Marquis de Custine, and even
the queen of Greece.

A little later, Balzac met the Marquise de Castries, who would
be a disappointed love and the cause of many sorrows, but who
nevertheless let him penetrate the Faubourg Saint-Germain
from her Hôtel de Castellane on Rue de Grenelle. Unlike the
Duchesse de Langeais, for whom she is said to be one of the
inspirations, the Marquise de Castries was not part of the high
nobility, and there is perhaps some truth in what Madame de
Villeparisis says about her – and about Balzac – in Proust's *By
Way of Sainte-Beuve*:

> What, above all, she could not stomach was that he should have
> laid claim to depict good society: 'To begin with, he never set foot
> in it, he was invited nowhere, what could he have known about it?
> Towards the end, he knew Mme de Castries, but he could not have
> seen anything of it in her house, she was a nobody. I once saw him
> there, just after I married, he was a very common sort of man,
> with nothing in particular to say, and I wouldn't have him intro-
> duced to me.'[2]

Balzac also frequented the salon of Sophie Gay, one of the
queens of Paris under the Directory, who entertained the literary elite in Rue Gaillon. The most beautiful ornament of the
place was her daughter Delphine, who married Émile de Girardin and had a salon in which Balzac was a familiar figure. She

played an important role in his life by calming the often tense relations between two difficult characters – her husband and her friend – and by bringing him into contact with Vigny, Lamartine, and many other celebrities. Among her many writings, she dedicated one to the author of *The Human Comedy*: 'La Canne de monsieur de Balzac', about a cane that has the property of making the person who carries it with his left hand invisible. ('M. Balzac hides in order to observe; he looks at people who think they are alone, as if no one had ever looked at them while they were thinking; he observes geniuses whom he catches as they jump out of bed, their feelings in their bathrobes, their vanities in their slippers, their fury in their hats, their misery in their jackets, and then he puts all these pieces of you in a book.')

Balzac also frequented the home of François Gérard, a famous portraitist (his *Madame Récamier* is famous to this day) who received guests on Wednesdays from midnight in his mezzanine at 6 Rue Saint-Germain-des-Prés (now Rue Bonaparte), almost opposite the church. It is likely that he met Stendhal there, when he had just published *Armance* and was preparing *Le Rouge et le Noir*. Around 1830 Balzac also became a regular at Charles Nodier's salon at the Arsenal on Sunday evenings. For him, *L'Histoire du roi de Bohème et ses sept châteaux* belonged to the 'school of disenchantment'. This was the beginning of a lasting friendship, as the long dedication of *The Wild Ass's Skin* testifies ('Perhaps your name will defend this work against the accusations it will receive').

After 1830, Balzac was no longer an unknown. His activities as a journalist had brought him into contact with the leading critics of the time, *The Physiology of Marriage* had won some renown, followed by *The Wild Ass's Skin*, which appeared, after the delays we have seen, with the greatest Romantic publisher, Charles Gosselin. Jules Janin would write in *La Caricature*:

> M. de Balzac has just put himself in the first rank of our story-tellers . . . You hear a great noise; people enter, people leave; people collide, people shout; people scream, people play; people get drunk; people are mad or foolish, are dead or tense; all scarred with blows, kisses, bites, voluptuousness, play, iron. That is the whole of *The Wild Ass's Skin*. It is the book of a brigand who lays in wait for you at the corner of a wood.[3]

'In the first rank of our storytellers': Balzac would now rub shoulders with the most famous writers. With some of them, a friendship was established; Balzac, if infernal with his publishers, was an attentive and sensitive friend. The list of dedicatees of *The Human Comedy* allows us to draw up a map of his literary relations with two names that emerge, two characters with whom Balzac regularly corresponded and even collaborated during the twenty or so years he had left to work: Théophile Gautier and George Sand.[4]

In 1836, Balzac, after reading Mademoiselle de Maupin, 'whose style he greatly admired', tried to contact Gautier to have him contribute to his new paper, *La Chronique de Paris*. Jules Sandeau went to look for him in his small flat in the Impasse du Doyenné and brought him to Rue Cassini. Gautier's description of this first meeting is well known:

> He wore from that time on, as a dressing gown, that white cash-mere or flannel robe held at the waist by a cord, in which, some time later, he had himself painted by Louis Boulanger . . . His

robe, thrown back, showed his athletic or bullish neck, round as a
section of a column, without visible muscles and of a satiny white-
ness which contrasted with the more coloured tone of his face . . .
His pure Touraine blood whipped his cheeks full of a lively crim-
son and warmly coloured his good thick and sinuous lips, which
readily laughed; a light moustache and a goatee accentuated the
contours without hiding them; the nose, square at the tip, divided
into two compartments and cut by well-opened nostrils, had a very
original and particular character; so Balzac, when posing for his
bust, recommended it to David d'Angers: 'Take care of my nose;
my nose is a world.' As for his eyes, there have never been any like
them. They had a life, a light, an inconceivable magnetism.[5]

From then on, a friendship developed. Thus, during a dinner
at Delphine de Girardin's, Gautier convinced Balzac to go to the
Hôtel Pimodan 'to take some hashish'. The next day, he wrote
to Madame Hanska: 'I resisted the hashish, and I did not experience all the phenomena; my brain is so strong that a stronger
dose was needed than the one I took.'[6] In *Artificial Paradises*,
Baudelaire, who was probably present at this session, tells it
differently:

I once observed him [Balzac] in a meeting where the spectacular
effects of hashish were under discussion. He listened and asked
questions with an amusing attention and intensity. Those who
knew him may guess how interested he must have been. But the
idea of thinking despite of himself shocked him to the core. He was
offered dawamesk; he examined it, sniffed at it, and returned it
without touching it. The struggle between his nearly childish curi-
osity and his repugnance for the act of abdication was betrayed on
his expressive face in a striking manner. His preference for dignity
won the day. In truth, though, it is hard to imagine the theoretician
of the *will*, that spiritual twin of Louis Lambert, consenting to lose
an ounce of that precious *substance*.[7]

Auguste Clésinger, *Théophile Gautier* (1853).

The friendship was coupled with a collaboration of writers. For *Lost Illusions* Gautier wrote the sonnet 'The Tulip' for Lucien de Rubempré's *Les Marguerites* (the sonnet 'The Camellia' is by Delphine de Girardin).

Balzac was not comfortable in versifying. In 1836, he wrote to Gautier: 'Since I saw you, I have fallen ill, but I have all the printed work at home today, won't you come and have dinner with me, to go over it all, there are two or three obscure places, where in a few minutes, we could put some light on it, come, I am in a hurry to have it corrected and printed.'[8]

It was to Gautier that Balzac addressed one of his last letters: 'I am given great hopes of recovery, but I must always remain in the state of a mummy, deprived of speech and movement; a state of affairs which must last at least a month. I owed this report to your friendship, which seems even more precious to me in the solitude in which the Faculty keeps me.'[9]

George Sand met Balzac in 1831. 'A friend of mine [certainly Sandeau] who knew a little of Balzac had introduced me to him, not as a "muse of the department", but as a good person from the provinces who was very amazed by his talent.'[10] She quickly fell under his spell: 'Oh! you would have understood the fascination of M. Balzac or you will never understand anything about the magic of the gaze and the sympathy of souls', she wrote to a friend.[11] A few years later, Balzac was George Sand's guest at her home in Berry:

> I reached the Château de Nohant on Saturday evening at about half past seven and found George Sand in her dressing gown smoking a cigar after dinner, by her fire, in a huge solitary room. She had pretty yellow slippers with tapered edges, smart stockings and red trousers . . . For three days we chatted from 5 p.m. until 5 a.m., so that I knew her more, and vice versa, in these three conversations than during the four previous years when she came to my house, when she loved Jules [Sandeau], and when she was linked with Musset, she met me or I went to her house from far and wide.[12]

It was George Sand who gave Balzac the idea for *Béatrix*, inspired by the love affair between Marie d'Agoult – a great friend of George's – and Franz Liszt.[13] Balzac portrays the character of Camille Maupin, the pen name of Félicité des Touches, with features clearly reminiscent of George Sand: she smokes cigarettes, she has a man's name, and dresses like a man. But he sprinkles the portrait with features that create a gap between the real character and the novelistic figure: 'Just as Clara Gazul is the female pseudonym of a distinguished male writer, George Sand the masculine pseudonym of a woman of genius, so Camille Maupin was the mask behind which was long hidden a charming young woman, very well-born, a Breton, named Félicité des Touches.'[14] Similarly, further on, Camille says to Calyste, the young hero of the novel: 'You have read as yet nothing of George Sand. I will send one of my people this very evening to Nantes to buy her works'; or again, 'while Calyste read *Indiana* – the first work by Camille's celebrated rival'.[15] This strategy of quoting the real character to prevent the fictional one from being too clearly assimilated to them would be used again by Proust, who evokes Anatole France or Sarah Bernhardt in the course of a sentence to prevent Bergotte and Berma from being too clearly perceived as portraits of these famous personalities. *Béatrix* would cause a chill in the friendship between George Sand and Marie d'Agoult, unhappy that the character who portrays her – Béatrix de Rochefide – is always inferior to Félicité des Touches, alias Camille Maupin. But the relationship between Balzac and George Sand was not shaken: 'My dear George, I had a good idea what was happening about Béatrix. Countless people interested in making us quarrel but who will never succeed sought to make you believe that Camille Maupin was a mischief on top of by several others.'[16] In fact, their relationship remained warm to the end and the last letter preserved is signed: 'A thousand tender and affectionate and gracious compliments from old Mar.'[17]

'Here, my dear Hugo, is the dedication of *Lost Illusions* that I am sending you in proof; I will come and see you next Friday at noon. To you from the heart.'[18] By dedicating to him what he considered a pillar of his work, Balzac shows the level at which he places Hugo among the writers of his time, yet his admiration was not without some annoyance – many others felt or would feel this way about Hugo, notably Baudelaire. In the 1840s, Hugo, a member of the Académie, a peer of France, and a friend of Louis-Philippe, was of a social rank incomparable with Balzac's, but this did not prevent a true friendship from developing between them. Hugo supported Balzac in his efforts to obtain the lifting of the ban on *Vautrin*. Balzac even asked him to help him correct passages in the play:

> My good and great Victor, I have just been struck by a horrible attack of fever on which the doctor has not yet ruled . . . As I know that Poets as high as you are lend their ideas as well as their money, please be so kind as to make a few cuts, mainly in the scene which ends the third act, and make the necessary changes so that Vautrin will be animated by a feeling of respect for his creation (Pygmalion for Galatea).[19]

And Hugo, for his part: 'Thank you, thank you in every way and for everything. Thank you for your beautiful genius, thank you for your loyal friendship.'[20] Balzac invited Hugo to dinner at the Rocher de Cancale, crossing Paris to visit him: 'Oh! we are getting old! My dear Hugo, I went to your house this morning, on the other side of the world from where I live, and I had the misfortune not to find you.'[21] Hugo supported Balzac's late candidacy for the Académie, visited him several times in his last days and in *Things Seen* described his friend's last moments:

> The candle barely lit the splendid furnishings of the salon and the magnificent paintings by Porbus and Holbein hanging on

the walls. The marble bust stood vaguely in this shadow like the
spectre of the man about to die . . . We passed through a corridor, went up a staircase covered with a red carpet and cluttered
with objets d'art, vases, statues, paintings, enamelled credenzas,
then another corridor, and I saw an open door. I heard a high,
sinister moan. I was in Balzac's room. In the middle of this room
was a bed. A mahogany bed with crossbars and straps at the foot
and head, indicating a support apparatus for moving the patient.
M. de Balzac was in this bed, his head resting on a pile of pillows
to which had been added red damask cushions borrowed from
the sofa in the room. His face was purple, almost black, slanted
to the right, his beard untrimmed, his hair grey and short, his
eyes open and fixed. I could see him in profile, and he looked
like the emperor . . . I went back downstairs, carrying this livid
figure in my thoughts; as I crossed the salon, I saw again the
immobile bust, impassive, haughty and vaguely radiant, and I
compared death to immortality.[22]

With Lamartine, another great glory of the time, the relationship was more one of mutual and strong admiration ('Dear and
illustrious poet, if the orator is not even greater . . .').[23] Balzac,
on the other hand, was very much at ease in his correspondence
with Nerval, Sue, Heine, or Marcelline Desbordes-Valmore; he
received foreigners such as Andersen or Alexander Humboldt;
in short, he was at the forefront of writers not only in France, but
also in the rest of Europe.

But he was not unanimously liked. Sainte-Beuve, invited by
Marie d'Agoult to a dinner party, refused to go because Balzac
would be there: 'You put me in mortal embarrassment; to dine
with Vautrin, that is to say to "eat salt" with him, is quite different from meeting him; it means shaking his hand, recanting,
confessing one's wrongs and promising there will be no more.

Thank you, thank you for that, I am not so good, so Christian.'[24] That evening, Balzac dined with Victor Hugo, Jean Auguste Dominque Ingres, and François Mignet.

Among the musicians of his time, Balzac's friends included Gioachino Rossini, to whom he dedicated *The Marriage Contract*; Franz Liszt, to whom *The Duchesse de Langeais* was dedicated and who served as the model for the character of Conti in *Béatrix*; and Hector Berlioz, dedicatee of *Ferragus*. Balzac failed to see the genius of Frédéric Chopin, whom he knew through George Sand – he only mentions in *A Man of Business* his talents as an imitator, his 'ability to counterfeit people', and would consider him as a piano teacher for Madame Hanska's daughter. Balzac was not a music lover like Stendhal; his tastes here were quite traditional. Like everyone else, he admired Eugène Delacroix, to whom he dedicated *The Girl with the Golden Eyes*, and Ingres, whom he would have liked to illustrate *The Human Comedy*. His favourite painters were Jacques-Louis David's pupils, such as Anne-Louis Girodet, whose 'Endymion' he particularly admired, and his friend François Gérard. He did not discern anything exceptional in Honoré Daumier, one illustrator for him among others, and if he mentions Théodore Géricault in *Pierre Grassou*, the great painter was drowned among Alexandre-Gabriel Descamps, Xavier Sigalon, and Eugène Deveria. There, as elsewhere, he remained classic in his tastes, and we never see him turn towards any form of the avant-garde of his time.

Those who might expect to find in *The Human Comedy* an accurate description of political life under the July monarchy will be disappointed. Indeed, we find the image of a city where, apart from the upheaval of July 1830, nothing happened – at least nothing in the streets: neither riots, nor uprisings, nor insur-rections. It is just in the turn of a sentence, in a quick allusion, that we sometimes perceive the distant echo of battles. Thus, on the first page of *The Seamy Side of History* (aka *The Brotherhood of Consolation*), where Godefroid dreams at the Pointe de la Cité: 'In 1836 this marvellous scene [the view of the Seine] presented still another lesson to the eye: between the Parisian leaning on the parapet and the cathedral lay the Terrain (such was the ancient name of this barren spot), still strewn with the ruins of the Archi-episcopal Palace.'[25] This is the only reference in *The Human Comedy* to the violent demonstrations in February 1831 following the celebration of a service in memory of the Duc de Berry at Saint-Germain-l'Auxerrois, which ended with the destruction of the archbishop's palace. In none of his novels does Balzac mention the riots during the trial of Charles X's ministers – despite, as we have seen, recounting these in the third of his *Lettres sur Paris*. Nor does he mention the cholera epidemic of the spring of 1832, so well described by his friend Heine (we only learn in *The False Mistress* that the Marquis de Ronquerolles lost his two children to the disease). As for the great republican revolt of 5 and 6 June 1832, it is only mentioned to tell how

> Horace Bianchon, Daniel d'Arthez, Léon Giraud, Joseph Bridau and Fulgence Ridal, despite the danger involved, went to move his body [that of Michel Chrestien, killed at Saint-Merry] in order to pay him their last respects in defiance of political fanaticism. During the night they accompanied these cherished remains to the cemetery of Père-Lachaise.[26]

Balzac was obviously aware of the dramatic events that shook Paris at the beginning of Louis-Philippe's reign, and if

he barely mentions them, it is because they are outside his subject. 'Writers who have a purpose in view', he wrote in his
Introduction to *The Human Comedy*, 'should always clear the
ground.' As none of his characters take part in the riot calling
for the death of the ministers, he does not mention it. When
Michel Chrestien is killed at Saint-Merry, Balzac recounts not
the battle, but the burial of this exemplary republican. It is not
a history of Paris he is writing but 'the seamy side of history',
an extraordinary title that he gave to one of his last books and
which shows the poetic precision this overweight man, exhausted
by illness, had reached.

The only significant event often mentioned in *The Human
Comedy* is the revolution of 1830 – not the days themselves but
their consequences.[27] During the Trois Glorieuses, Balzac was
in Saché at the home of M. de Margonne. 'I consider myself', he
writes in the first *Lettre sur Paris*, 'a very brave man to admit that
I was travelling on the banks of the Indre during our glorious
days.' Others would have rushed back to Paris, but not him: he
stayed in the country and did not return until September –
strange behaviour for the journalist he was then. From La
Grenadière, he wrote to a friend:

> Oh, if you only knew what Touraine is like! One forgets everything
> here. I forgive the inhabitants for being stupid, they are so
> happy! . . . I have come to look upon glory, the Chamber, politics,
> the future, literature, as mere pellets to kill stray and homeless
> dogs, and I say: Virtue, happiness, life, is six hundred francs'
> income from government bonds on the banks of the Loire.[28]

However, Balzac repeatedly describes the upheaval in Parisian life caused by the July Days, the shift in power from the

nobility of the Faubourg Saint-Germain to the bankers of the Chaussée-d'Antin. Sometimes he himself speaks in one of his customary interpolations; sometimes he entrusts this to a character, such as the friend Raphaël met near the Pont des Arts when leaving the shop where he bought the wild ass's skin:

> The infamous monarchy which has been overthrown by popular heroism was a woman of loose life with whom one could banquet and make merry; but our country itself is a virtuous – not to say shrewish – spouse. We must, whether we will or not, put up with her frigid caresses. So here we are: political power has been transferred from the Tuileries Palace to the newspaper offices, just as economic power has changed its address from the Faubourg Saint-Germain to the Chaussée d'Antin. But here's something you perhaps don't know: the government, that is to say, the aristocracy of bankers and barristers who today pay lip-service to patriotism as formerly the priests to monarchism, sees the need to hoodwink the good people of France with new words for old ideas, after the example of the philosophers of every school and the hard-headed men of all times. And so it's a question of inculcating in us a royally national point of view by proving to us that we are much happier paying twelve hundred millions and thirty-three centimes to the country, represented by Messrs So-and-So, than eleven hundred millions and nine centimes to a king who said *I* instead of *we*.[29]

Balzac is often described as a defender of throne and altar, and not without reason: 'I write under the light of two eternal Truths: Religion and Monarchy, two necessities, as they are shown by contemporary events, towards which every writer of sound sense ought to try to guide the country back,' he writes in his Introduction. But what throne and what altar are we talking about? The answer is not simple.

To start with the altar: on countless occasions, Balzac praises the Catholic religion, but what it represents for him is a means of maintaining the social order. As the Duchesse de Langeais explains to the unbelieving Montriveau: 'Religion, Armand, is, you see, the bond uniting all conservative principles that enable the rich to live peacefully. Religion is intimately bound to property. It is certainly finer to lead people by moral ideas than by scaffolds, as in the time of the Terror, the only means that your detestable revolution had invented to instil obedience.'[30] Besides, it cannot be said that Balzac was devout: he only went to church for weddings and funerals, and he often insists on the evils of religious bigotry, as in his account of the childhood of Marie-Angélique and Marie-Eugénie, the two daughters of the Comtesse de Granville, 'brought up in a gloomy house in the Marais, by a woman of narrow mind, a "*dévote*"', whose education 'did not go beyond the limits imposed by confessors, who were chosen by their mother from the strictest and the least tolerant of Jansenist priests'.[31]

Just as Balzac's Catholicism was more utilitarian than mystical, so his loyalty to the throne varied according to who occupied it. There is, however, one constant in his political vision: the social hierarchy must be strict, based on property and maintained with an iron fist. He wrote to his friend Zulma Carraud:

France must be a constitutional monarchy, should have a hereditary royal family, an extremely powerful Chamber of Peers, which represents property . . . then a second elective assembly which represents all the interests of the intermediate mass, separating the high social positions from what I call the people. The greater part of laws and their spirit should tend to enlighten the people as much as possible, the people who have nothing, the workers, proletarians, etc., in order to bring as many men as possible to the state of ease that distinguishes the intermediate mass. But the people should also be kept under the most powerful yoke, which should have all power so that individuals can find light, support, wealth and protection, and that no idea, no form, no transaction should make them turbulent . . . Thus government, the rich and the bourgeois have an interest in making the lowest class happy and enlarging the middle class where the real power of the states lies.

Zulma Carraud was truly a good friend of Balzac; though admiring him, she stood up to him:

> You set up as a principle the necessity of social classifications, want to sort the human species according to the chances of birth and condemn to bitter servitude, to degrading dependence, people with broad ideas, with a genius equal to yours, perhaps. I saw here a tribute to your party, and a sigh came painfully from my chest. I said to myself: if Honoré, born a cobbler, had been condemned to make boots, in spite of the creative fire he had felt bubbling up inside him![32]

That Balzac was always a friend of order did not prevent him from varying his position with regard to the government. Under the Restoration, he was on the side of what was then called liberalism, that is, support for the constitutional monarchy against the ultra-royalists. He admired Napoleon, who was regarded at the time as the son of the Revolution – the parade of the Grande Armée in front of the Tuileries at the beginning of *A Woman of Thirty* is described with a kind of fervour.[33] In *The Chouans* (1829), the first of the novels in *The Human Comedy*, the republican soldiers, the *bleus* commanded by Hulot, are portrayed as civilized beings, unlike Chouans such as the terrible Marche-à-terre, a man 'chopped out, as it seemed as by an axe, with his rough bark still left on him', while 'the stupid ignorance of his features made him seem, for the moment, like some half-savage demigod'.[34] According to Roger Pierrot, Balzac even corrected the text of the definitive edition published in 1845 to erase aspects that were too 'Jacobin'. And we often find in his work characters described in favourable colours despite their 'advanced' ideas – such as Pillerault, Madame Birotteau's benevolent uncle, who 'enlivened his old age with his political convictions, which, let us say, were those of the extreme left'.

After the days of July 1830, Balzac analysed the errors of the aristocracy on which the throne of the last Bourbons rested:

> The Faubourg Saint-Germain played with batons, believing that they were power itself. It reversed the terms of the proposition that called it into existence. Instead of throwing away the insignia that offended the people and quietly retaining its power, it allowed the bourgeoisie to seize authority, clung so fatally to its insignia, and constantly again forgot the laws that its numerical weakness decreed . . . Instead of acting protector, like a great man, the Faubourg Saint-Germain was as greedy as an upstart. When the most intelligent nation in the world understood that the restored nobility had organized power and the budget to its own profit, it fell mortally ill.[35]

But Balzac is even harsher towards the regime that emerged from the July Revolution. 'The disasters of July 1830 came, society was dissolved for two years', he writes in *A Daughter of Eve*; and time and again he expresses his dislike of what Paris had become under Louis-Philippe – the reign of lawyers, bankers and journalists, the Nucingens, Du Tillets, and Finots. 'Society on its grand scale has been demolished to make a million of little ones in the image of the defunct. These parasitic organizations reveal decomposition; are they not the swarming of maggots in the dead body?'[36]

In the early 1830s, Balzac got to know the Duc de Fitz-James, leader of the Carlist party; he assiduously frequented the salon of the Austrian ambassador and became a legitimist to the point of considering running for election under this flag.[37] But, at the same time, he made connections in very different circles. His friend Princesse Belgioso suggested that he should collaborate with *La Démocratie pacifique*, 'a good newspaper, still young and not flashy, which often contains excellent background articles', she told him.[38] It was in fact a Fourierist newspaper whose director was Victor Considérant, the most left-wing figure of the legal opposition. Balzac also corresponded with Toussenel, another far-left publicist, who wrote to him: 'The disciples of Fourier owe you a great debt of gratitude for the accuracy with which you have explained the system of their master.'[39]

A distanced Catholic, subject of an unobtainable king, Balzac's coherence is not to be found here, but rather in what seemed to him 'at first a dream, one of those impossible projects which we caress and then let fly; a chimera that us a glimpse of its smiling woman's face, and forthwith spreads its wings and returns to a heavenly realm', as he wrote in his Introduction to *The Human Comedy*.

The beginning of *Facino Cane*, a short story from 1836, is written in an unusual autobiographical mode:

At the time, I was living on a little street you probably do not know, Rue de Lesdiguières. It starts at Rue Saint-Antoine across from a fountain near Place de la Bastille, and ends at Rue de la Cerisaie . . . In fine weather I would at most take a brief stroll on Boulevard Bourdon. There was only one activity that could draw me away from my studious routine, although this was virtually part of the same passion: I would walk about observing the customs of the neighbourhood, its inhabitants and their character. As poorly dressed as the workmen themselves, careless about decorum, I never put them on their guard . . . on some nights between eleven and midnight, I would come across a workman and his wife on their way home from the Ambigu-Comique music hall, and I would spend some time following them from Boulevard [now Rue] du Pont-aux-Choux to Boulevard Beaumarchais. These good folk would be chatting about the show they had just seen; eventually they would get around to talking about their work . . . Listening to these people, I could join in their lives: I would feel their rags on my back, I would be walking in their tattered shoes; their desires, their longings, their needs would all the more move through my soul, or my soul through theirs.

A little further on, the narrator recounts the wedding of his housekeeper's sister:

I meant to nestle into the happiness of these poor folks. Both the ceremony and the festivities took place at the warehouse of a wine merchant on Rue Charenton, one floor up in a large hall lit by tin reflector lamps; the walls were hung with filthy paper at table level and lined with wooden benches. Inside the room some eighty people gathered in their Sunday best, with flowers and ribbons all around, everyone soaring with the nightlife spirit of the dance halls at La Courtille; their faces flaming, they danced as if the world was about to end.[40]

These pages are an exception: there is no other example in *The Human Comedy* of a striking scene in a working-class environment. Here and there we meet workers, but only in passing – as at the beginning of *Ferragus*, where Auguste de Maulincour, absorbed in the contemplation of the house into which he has seen the woman he loves enter, heard a voice that said: '"Hi, there," and the young man was conscious of a blow on the shoulder. "Why don't you pay attention," said the rough voice of a workman, carrying a plank on his shoulder. The man passed on.'[41] Balzac might well assert that 'from that time [that of *Facino Cane*] I had broken down the elements of this heterogeneous mass called the people, I had analysed it in such a way as to be able to evaluate its good or bad qualities' – but the fact remains that the people are the great absentee of *The Human Comedy*. The people and their neighbourhoods, because Balzac's characters, whether bourgeois or aristocratic, have no business in the working-class suburbs. If the Faubourg Saint-Marceau is an important site in *Colonel Chabert*, Balzac hardly visits the Faubourg Saint-Antoine apart from in *Facino Cane*. There is a brief allusion to its political role when Mother Madou, the hazelnut seller, bursts into César Birotteau's house to claim her due, 'like an insurrection of the Faubourg Saint-Antoine'; and a remark about the vernacular of Atala Judici, one of Baron Hulot's latest conquests, who lives on Rue de Charonne: 'The people of the Faubourg Saint-Antoine never call this famous district anything other than the faubourg. It is for them the faubourg par excellence.' As for the Faubourg du Temple, we know that Birotteau built his workshops there, but they are no more described than the faubourg itself, or than Rue Saint-Maur, where Honorine lives, as well as the little Olympe Bijou, another member of the great Hulot tribe.

The only place in eastern Paris that comes up several times in *The Human Comedy* is the Père-Lachaise cemetery. On these heights we witness Rastignac's famous challenge at the end of *Old Man Goriot*, as well as the clandestine burial of Michel Chrestien by his friends of the Cénacle in the wake of the Saint-Merry riot, and the funeral of Ferragus's daughter, whose coffin is followed by twelve strangers, each in a carriage draped in black, to the top of the cemetery.

During the years of *The Human Comedy*, the face of Paris changed, especially on the Right Bank from the arc of the boulevards to the city wall. In this large area, hitherto sparsely populated, as we have seen, new districts were built: the extension of the Chaussée-d'Antin; Nouvelle Athènes; the Notre-Dame-de-Lorette and Saint-Georges quarters; and the Quartier d'Europe. It became the liveliest, most amusing, richest (*nouveau riche* if you like), most artistic area of Paris – and the epicentre of *The Human Comedy*. But this New Paris of Balzac's was not the only upheaval in the city: other major works were being undertaken at the time, which Balzac hardly ever mentions. In *Béatrix*, for example, the Quartier de l'Europe is described at length, but there is no mention of the Saint-Lazare railway station, a sensational new construction built on the Place de l'Europe and the terminus of France's first railway line, the Paris-Saint-Germain.[42] Recall that Balzac himself took the train to Paris from Les Jardies – 'for 8 sous and in fifteen or twenty minutes, I am in Paris.' Nor is there any mention of the Embacadère de Strasbourg (the Gare de l'Est) from which his friend Nerval took the train to Meaux at the end of *October*

Nights. In *The Human Comedy*, there is nothing about the stations and railways that were beginning to mark the city with their cuttings, glass roofs, and metalwork. Nothing, except this prediction in the first lines of *A Start in Life* (1842): 'Railroads, in a future not far distant, must force certain industries to disappear forever, and modify several others, more especially those relating to the different modes of transport in use around Paris.'[43]

Another major construction project not mentioned in *The Human Comedy* is the fortifications built in the early 1840s outside the Wall of the Farmers-General, which de facto incorporated into the city previously independent communes such as Montmartre, Auteuil, and Belleville.[44] These works may well have been peripheral, but they certainly had an impact on the life of central Paris, through the movement of people, the carting of materials, and the flow of workers from all over the provinces. Balzac would show the site of these works to Lirette, Madame Hanska's Polish schoolteacher: 'I took her yesterday to the fortifications, and she was stunned to see 88 counterscarps, a wall 40 feet high, built as if from a single block, and two superb roads, planted with trees, inside and outside the fortifications. It is as pretty as a mirror, the stones are as if set in Roman cement.'[45] But in *The Human Comedy*, unless I am mistaken, we find no reference to these gigantic works.[46]

Balzac therefore left out whole sections, political and urban, of the Paris of his time. This is because *The Human Comedy* is neither a history of the city nor an investigation according to the rules of sociology, a science whose name emerged in the year in which *A Great Man in Embryo*, the second part of *Lost Illusions*, was published (1839). The legend of a realistic and documentary work was created by Balzac himself, who insisted in both his Introduction and his prefaces on his concern for exhaustiveness and accuracy. Since then, this legend has persisted as a matter of course, relayed in particular by Marxist critics who, from Engels to Lukács, have praised Balzac's realism.

In his inaugural lecture at the Collège de France, Louis Chevalier said that 'this work [of Balzac] has all the aspects of a historical document. The conviction of authenticity that reading these books imposes on the historian results far less from the meticulous description of certain privileged districts, or from the major characters of *The Human Comedy*, than from the multiple links that unite these districts with the whole city and these characters with society as a whole.' Balzac's 'conviction of authenticity' is felt above all in the two themes that recur like a leitmotif in the first pages of *The Girl with the Golden Eyes*: money and pleasure. On money, Balzac's documentary accuracy is unparalleled, based on his personal experience – his years as a notary's clerk, the bankruptcy of his printing business, his countless financial mishaps, his risky speculations. Thus we have the controversy between the two notaries in *The Marriage Contract*, the unfolding of César Birotteau's bankruptcy, and the origins of the Nucingen fortune detailed by Blondet in *The Firm of Nucingen*: all descriptions so precise and detailed that today's reader can sometimes get lost in them. Money itself is magnified by Gobseck in astonishing pages where it 'represents all human forces'. It was this lucidity about capitalism from the inside that made Marxists enthusiastic about Balzac (before the appearance of Livre de Poche in 1953, you could buy Balzac's works in Soviet editions, on bad paper but very cheap).

Ferragus (Daumier,
Édition Furne)

The 'multiple links' that Louis Chevalier speaks of are woven
between places and an immense population. Balzac himself
writes in his Introduction: 'It was no small task to paint the two
or three thousand salient figures of an era, for such is, in the final
analysis, the sum of the types that each generation presents and
that *The Human Comedy* will include.' For once, he was not
exaggerating: *The Human Comedy* has two thousand five
hundred characters, and the index of fictional characters occupies more than four hundred pages in the Pléiade edition. While
those who first come to mind may be Gaudissart or Antoinette
de Langeais, Diane de Maufrigneuse or César Birotteau, Carlos

Herrera or Ferragus, these figures only acquire their full vividness by being drawn from a world built on the mass of secondary characters. Not only are these portrayed with as much care as the Rastignacs and de Marsays, but they often allow Balzac to open up strange worlds. For example, Father Canquoëlle, a pillar of the Café David – with his veneered steel buckled shoes, his snowy, powdered head, who 'seemed so perfectly in harmony with the righteous people gathered here that no one ventured to talk politics in his presence' – concealed behind this reassuring outward appearance a terrible spy named Peyrade, who plays a major role in the thrilling dénouement of *A Harlot High and Low*. Balzac draws the reader into a description of the police in the latter days of the Empire and the reign of Louis XVIII, when Peyrade was a special agent of the monarch. Similarly, in *The False Mistress*, we enter the world of the circus with Malaga, the beautiful horsewoman, or the world of hairdressers with Bixiou and de Lora in *The Unconscious Comedians*. These passages are not parentheses or digressions but the cement that holds together the materials of the Balzac edifice. In this essential role of secondary characters, one can see a common thread between *The Human Comedy* and the great American cinema. Their profusion helps to create the sense of energy that Baudelaire noted:

> All his characters are endowed with the vital ardour with which he himself was inspired. All his fictions are as deeply coloured as dreams. From the summit of the aristocracy to the lower depths of the plebs, all the actors in his *Comedy* are fiercer in life, more active and cunning in struggle, more patient in misfortune, more gullible in enjoyment, more angelic in devotion, than the comedy of the real world shows them to us.[47]

The Human Comedy is not the comedy of the real world, as Balzac's poetic imagination often overrides documentary accuracy. Thus, his Parisian society is overpopulated with blondes – Béatrix, Honorine, Paquita (the 'girl with the golden eyes'), Antoinette de Langeais, Florine, Diane de Maufrigneuse, Hortense Hulot, Madame de Mortsauf ... Also blond young men – Lucien de Rubempré, Raphaël in *The Wild Ass's Skin*, and Arthur, the lover in *A Woman of Thirty* (who is admittedly English). And when hair is dark it is always jet-black, like that of the beautiful Josépha Mirah, 'black and shiny as satin', or 'blue black', like Esther's. As for chestnut hair, probably the most common then as now, it is absent from *The Human Comedy*.

After the long introduction of *The Girl with the Golden Eyes* – written in grey tones for a work dedicated to Delacroix, in which the red, white, and gold of *The Death of Sardanapalus* abound – when Balzac tires of detailing each layer of the Parisian population, he lets rip:

> But, oh Paris! He who has not admired your gloomy passages, your gleams and flashes of light, your deep and silent cul-de-sacs, who has not listened to your murmurings between midnight and two in the morning, knows nothing as yet of your true poesy, nor of your broad and fantastic contrasts. There are a few amateurs who never go their way heedlessly; who savour their Paris, so to speak; who know its physiognomy so well that they see every wart and pimple and blemish. To others, Paris is always that monstrous marvel, that amazing assemblage of activities, of schemes, of thoughts; the city of a hundred thousand tales, the head of the universe.[48]

Balzac is no more of a realist than Scheherazade, himself often evoking the example of the *Thousand and One Nights*. As

Baudelaire wrote: 'I have often been astonished that Balzac's great fame was that of a visionary, and a passionate one.'[49] If I absolutely had to find an adjective for Balzac's Paris, I would choose 'modern', though he rarely uses it: 'There is more than one street in Paris where such a meeting may lead to a frightful drama, a bloody drama of death and love, a drama of the modern school.'[50] But we already find in *The Human Comedy* the 'heroism of modern life', this way of showing 'how great and poetic we are in our ties and our patent boots', as Baudelaire wrote at the end of *The Salon of 1845*. At the same time, Théophile Gautier also noted how 'many criticisms have been made of Balzac and there are many ways of talking about him; but one point has not been emphasised, which in our opinion is very characteristic: this point is the absolute modernity of his genius'. His contemporaries saw this clearly (perhaps better than we do): Balzac was the creator of the modern novel, the painter of the modern city, he occupies the central Parisian place between Rousseau, Diderot, and Restif, on the one hand, and Baudelaire, Apollinaire, and Breton on the other.

You do not emerge unscathed from a deep dive into Balzac's Paris, for how can you pass through Rue Cassette without a thought for Carlos Herrera, avoid in Rue Taitbout the ghost of Esther, or ascend Rue Tournefort without furtively looking for the Maison Vauquer? You are contaminated, and in the most serious cases you sometimes make untimely connections: Malaga, the beautiful horsewoman who 'can dismount and remount on a horse at full gallop', suggests Degas and 'Miss La La at the Cirque Fernando'; the wooden façade of The Cat and Racket suggests the barns in Alabama photographed by Walker Evans; the interior of the Café David the bistro lit by Coutard in

Jean-Luc Godard's *Two or Three Things I Know About Her*. At the time of writing (March 2017), the Paris Opéra is staging the work of an Italian composer, Luca Francesconi, entitled *Trompe-la-Mort*, with its hero Vautrin.

Balzac's relationship with Paris is unique. Other great authors have written about Rome, Berlin, or London, as well as Paris, but none of them would have dared to say anything like this: 'For me, there are memories at every door, thoughts at every lamppost. Not a façade has been built, not a building knocked down, but that I have not spied on its birth or death. I take part in the immense movement of this world as if I had its soul.'

And the great Balzac continues, even more imperially: 'The birch trees are mine, the shade of the Tuileries is mine, the lilacs of the Luxembourg, the young colonnades of the Palais-Royal are mine. Ah! No one will know so well as I do the delicious hours when Paris falls asleep, when the last roll of a coach resounds, when the songs of companions cease.'[51]

'No one will know so well as I do' – a remarkable prediction, a magnificent megalomania – and history would prove him right.

Notes

Why Paris?

1. *Le Mendiant*, a short text dating from 1830, in *Oeuvres diverses*, vol. 2 (Paris: Gallimard, 1996), p. 1123. This also contains a panorama of Paris reprised in the chapter 'The Finger of God', in *A Woman of Thirty*.
2. *The Girl with the Golden Eyes*, trans. Ellen Marriage (Project Gutenberg ebook, 2010), loc. 178985.
3. *Petty Troubles of Married Life* (Project Gutenberg ebook, 2005), loc. 194466.
4. *Le Mendiant*, p. 1123.

A Wanderer

1. Currently no. 122. At the beginning of *Louis Lambert*, Balzac describes life at the Collège de Vendôme at length. 'Once entered there, a pupil never leaves till his studies are finished. With the exception of walks taken under the guidance of the Fathers, everything is calculated to give the School the benefit of convent discipline; in my day the tawse was still a living memory, and the

classical leather strap played its terrible part with all the honours', trans. Clara Bell and James Waring (Project Gutenberg ebook, 2010), loc. 160120.

2. Today it houses the Musée Picasso.

3. *Correspondance* I (Paris: Gallimard, 2006), p. 4.

4. The location corresponds to 37 and 39 Rue de Turenne.

5. *Louis Lambert*, loc. 76438. Les Frères Provençaux was one of the two major restaurants in the Palais-Royal, the other being Véry.

6. 'Facino Cane', trans. Linda Asher in *The Human Comedy: Selected Stories*, ed. Peter Brooks (New York: New York Review Books, 2014), p. 3. The building was located in the part of the street destroyed by the construction of Boulevard Henri IV. Monsieur's library was that of the Arsenal.

7. January 1846, in *Lettres à Madame Hanska*, vol. 2 (Paris: Laffont, 1990), p. 146.

8. Raphael is describing his room at the Hôtel de Cluny. *The Wild Ass's Skin*, trans. Herbert J. Hunt (London: Penguin 1977), p. 109.

9. The building on Rue du Roi Doré still exists. Rue de Berry has been incorporated into Rue Charlot.

10. This beautiful neoclassical building still exists.

11. *Correspondance* I, p. 149. *Wann-Chlore* is a novel written under the name of Saint-Aubin.

12. Rue des Marais is now Rue Visconti. The buildings of the print shop still exist. Balzac lived in a tiny flat near his workplace.

13. Letter to Géneral Baron de Pommereul, in *Correspondance* I, p. 220.

14. Théophile Gautier, *Balʒac* (Paris: Le Castor Astral, 1999), pp. 57–8. Rue des Batailles disappeared with the construction of Avenue d'Iéna.

15. *Letttres à Madame Hanska*, vol. 1, p. 456.

16. For failing to fulfil his obligations to the Garde Nationale, Balzac spent a few days in the 'Hôtel des Haricots', the prison for draft dodgers.

17. *Lettres à Madame Hanska*, vol. 1, p. 490. The Paris-Versailles 'Right Bank' line opened in August 1839. It left from the Gare

Saint-Lazare, then located in the former Tivoli gardens, now Place de l'Europe.

18. Rue Basse was widened to become the present Rue Raynouard. Rue du Roc, which is more or less unchanged, is now the pretty Rue Berton. This building is now the Maison de Balzac, a museum and library.

19. *Correspondance* IV, p. 769.

20. *Archives nationales, Minutier central des notaires*, quoted in Roger Pierrot, *Honoré de Balzac* (Paris: Fayard, 1994), p. 445.

The Street

1. *Ferragus, Chief of the Devorants*, trans. by Katharine Prescott Wormeley (Project Gutenberg ebook, 2010), loc. 90610. Rue Traversière-Saint-Honoré joined Rue Saint-Honoré and Rue de Richelieu obliquely, across the Butte des Moulins, a centre of prostitution. It disappeared with the construction of Avenue de l'Opéra. Rue Fromenteau was located in the Carrousel district; Rue Pagevin was close to the Place des Victoires.

2. *Another Study of Womankind*, trans. Jordan Stump in *The Human Comedy: Selected Stories*, ed. Peter Brooks (New York: New York Review Books, 2014), p. 38.

3. Louis Sébastien Mercier, *Tableau de Paris*, p. 46.

4. Eugène Sue, *Les Mystères de Paris* (Paris: Jean-Jacques Pauvert, 1963), p. 2. The action of the book, published in sheet form in 1842, takes place in 1838.

5. 'Mists and Rains' (*Les Fleurs du mal*) and 'Loss of Halo' (*Poems in Prose*).

6. The system of sewers doubling the depth of each Parisian street dates from the work of Eugène Belgrand in the 1850s.

7. *Cousin Pons*, trans. Herbert J. Hunt (London: Penguin, 1968), p. 248.

8. Respectively in *Cousin Pons, Rise and Fall of César Birotteau, A Second Home, The Commission in Lunacy*. Rue du Tourniquet-Saint-Jean was part of a network of alleys behind the Hôtel de Ville, the

destruction of which began in Balzac's time. Rue de Normandie and Rue du Fouarre still exist.

9. *Old Man Goriot*, trans. Catherine McCannon (London: Penguin, 2011), pp. 51–2.

10. *At the Sign of the Cat and Racket*, trans. Clara Bell (Project Gutenberg ebook, 2010), loc. 104706.

11. *The Wild Ass's Skin*, trans. Herbert J. Hunt (London: Penguin 1977), p. 136.

12. *Lost Illusions*, trans. Herbert J. Hunt (London: Penguin 1971), p. 261. Chevet was a famous (real) caterer, who appears many times in *The Human Comedy*.

13. *A Harlot High and Low*, trans. Rayner Heppenstall (London: Penguin, 1970), p. 306.

14. Rue du Martroi was part of the network of alleys behind the Hôtel de Ville.

15. *A Harlot High and Low*, p. 307.

16. *Gobseck*, trans. Ellen Marriage (Project Gutenberg ebook, 2010), loc. 37219.

17. *Old Man Goriot*, pp. 43–4.

18. *The Duchesse de Langeais*, trans. Carol Cosman, in *The Human Comedy: Selected Stories*, ed. Peter Brooks (New York: New York Review Books, 2014), p. 387.

19. *A Harlot High and Low*, p. 64.

20. In 1826, there were 2,100 fiacres and cabriolets in Paris, which charged 1.50 F inside the barriers – or an hourly rate of 2.25 F for the fiacres and 1.50 F for the cabriolets. See Bertier de Sauvigny, *La France sous la Restoration* (Paris: Armand Colin, 1955), p. 206. The first omnibus company was founded in 1828. It ran 100 carriages on ten lines that departed from the Bastille (to Bercy, Place du Trône, Place du Carrousel, Porte Saint-Martin), the Madeleine (to the Bastille and the Barrière des Bons Hommes (now Quai de New York), and from Quai Conti (to the village of Gros-Caillou, the Jardin du Roi (now Jardin des Plantes), Place du Carrousel, the Barrière des Ternes). Its success had already given rise to a number of competing companies, such as the Dames Blanches, the

Écossaises, the Béarnaises, the Carolines, the Batinolaises. See Marc
Gaillard, *Histoire des transports parisiens de Blaise Pascal à nos jours*
(Paris: Horvath, n.d.).

21. Léon Gozlan, *Balzac en pantoufles* (Paris: Maisonneuve et Larose,
2001 (1862)), p. 26. Roger Pierrot's biography suggests that Gozlan
did not know Balzac as well as he says he did, but he can probably be
trusted on coffee.

22. *Ferragus*, loc. 90587.

23. *A Harlot High and Low*, p. 34.

24. On all these points, see the 'Lumières' chapter of Simone Delattre's
excellent book *Les Douze Heures noires, la nuit à Paris au XIXe siècle*
(Paris: Albin Michel, 2000).

25. *A Start in Life*, trans. Katharine Prescott Wormeley (Project Gutenberg ebook, 2010), loc. 37976.

26. The text appeared in a book published by Hetzel in 1845–6, *Le
Diable à Paris, Mœurs et coutumes, caractères et portraits des habitants
de Paris, tableau complet de leur vie privée, publique, politique, artis-
tique, littéraire, industrielle*. The work, illustrated with vignettes by
Granville, Gavarni, and Nanteuil, includes texts by George Sand,
Musset, Nerval, and Nodie. In addition to *Ce qui disparaît de Paris*,
Balzac published in it *The Physiology of Marriage* and *Petty Troubles
of Married Life*.

27. Victor Hugo, 'Guerre aux démolisseurs', pamphlet published in the
Revue des Deux Mondes, 1832.

Quarters

1. *Gobseck*, p. 230. In this house, Gobseck has as a neighbour Derville,
to whom he lends the money necessary to buy his office of solicitor.
Rue des Grès extended between Rue Saint-Jacques and Rue de la
Harpe, more or less on the current route of Rue Cujas. The expression *jour de souffrance* [more literally 'borrowed light'] is often used
in *The Human Comedy*.

2. *Paz*, trans. Katharine Prescott Wormeley (Project Gutenberg ebook,
2010), loc. 30639.

3. In *Rise and Fall of César Birotteau* and *Cousin Pons*. The elegant Rue Basse-du-Rempart ran from Place de la Madeleine to Rue de la Chaussée-d'Antin below Boulevard de la Madeleine. The Foreign Ministry and the Austrian Embassy were located here.

4. *Honorine*, trans. Clara Bell (Project Gutenberg ebook, 2010).

5. *A Harlot High and Low*, p. 96.

6. *The Collection of Antiquities*, trans. Ellen Marriage (Project Gutenberg ebook, 2010), loc. 41185.

7. L. Gozlan, *Balzac en pantoufles*, pp. 109–10.

8. *Ferragus*, loc. 176768.

9. *The Commission in Lunacy*, trans. Clara Bell (Gutenberg Project ebook, 2010), loc. 42819-20.

10. *Old Man Goriot*. p. 4. Rue Neuve-Sainte-Genevieve is now Rue Tournefort.

11. Walter Benjamin, *The Arcades Project* (Cambridge, MA: The Belknap Press, 2002), p. 83.

12. In *The Commission in Lunacy*.

13. *Lost Illusions*, p. 329.

14. The street that became Rue Laffitte after 1830.

15. *Lost Illusions*, p. 188. 'A Great Man in Embyro' is the second part of the novel. Rue de Cluny ran from Rue des Grès to Place de la Sorbonne, the present route of Rue Victor-Cousin.

16. Ibid., p. 190. The three churches are difficult to identify: obviously the Sorbonne chapel, but the other two?

17. Ibid., pp. 205, 207.

18. Rue des Cordiers ran between Rue de Cluny and Rue Saint-Jacques. Rousseau did indeed live in the Hôtel Saint-Quentin; he mentions it in his *Confessions*.

19. *The Wild Ass's Skin*, p. 109.

20. 'Z. Marcas', trans. Linda Asher, in *The Human Comedy: Selected Stories*, ed. Peter Brooks (New York: New York Review Books, 2014), p. 209.

21. Ibid., pp. 216–17.

22. This is now Rue Champollion. It has not changed much since then, apart from the cinemas.

23. *Lost Illusions*, pp. 193 and 195.

24. *Colonel Chabert*, trans. Ellen Marriage and Clara Bell (Project Gutenberg ebook, 2010), loc. 164688–9.

25. *Colonel Chabert*, loc. 194898. Rue du Petit-Banquier corresponds roughly to the present Rue Watteau.

26. Ibid., loc. 164901ff.

27. *A Woman of Thirty*, trans. Ellen Marriage (Project Gutenberg ebook, 2010), loc. 163353ff.

28. 'The Duchesse de Langeais', trans. Carol Cosman, in *The Human Comedy: Selected Stories*, ed. Peter Brooks (New York: New York Review Books, 2014), p. 302.

29. In, respectively, *At the Sign of the Cat and Racket*, *A Second Home*, *The Duchesse de Langeais*.

30. Rue de Bourbon became Rue de Lille, and Rue Plumet, Rue Oudinot.

31. *The Duchesse de Langeais*, p. 301.

32. Marcel Proust, *The Guermantes Way*, vol. 1 of *Remembrance of Things Past*, trans. C. K. Scott Moncrieff (London: Penguin, 1989), p. 25.

33. 'The Duchesse de Langeais', pp. 305–8.

34. Ibid., pp. 388–9.

35. *Correspondance* III (Paris: Garnier 1962ff.), p. 55.

36. In an article for the *New Monthly Magazine*, quoted by Henri Martineau in his review of *Armance*. See Stendhal, *Oeuvres romanesques complètes* (Paris: Gallimard, 2005), vol. 1, p. 14.

37. Baudelaire, 'Théophile Gautier', in *Curiosités esthétiques* (Paris: Garnier, 1999), p. 679.

38. Alfrez Delvau, *Histoire anecdotique des cafés et cabarets de Paris* (Paris: Dentu, 1862), p. 197.

39. *The Black Sheep*, trans. Donald Adamson (London: Penguin, 1970), p. 38.

40. *A Daughter of Eve*, trans. Katharine Prescott Wormeley (Project Gutenberg ebook, 2010), loc. 63684.

41. *The Atheist's Mass*, trans. Clara Bell (Project Gutenberg ebook, 2010), loc. 3530.

42. *Lost Illusions*, pp. 218–19.

43. Today the maternity hospital of Port-Royal.

44. *Lost Illusions*, p. 336. Rue de l'Ouest is now Rue d'Assas.

45. *The Brotherhood of Consolation*, trans. Katharine Prescott Wormeley (Project Gutenberg ebook, 2010), loc. 172082.

46. As we have seen, Rue des Marais-Saint-Germain is the present Rue Visconti.

47. For Balzac's relations with his publishers, see below, p. 114 ff. Rue Saint-Germain-des-Prés corresponds to the upper part of Rue Bonaparte.

48. *The Brotherhood of Consolation*, loc. 170317. Sainte-Geneviève is now the Panthéon. The Hôtel-Dieu spanned both arms of the Seine, its two parts connected by the Pont au Double.

49. *Histoire et physiologie des boulevards de Paris*, text published in *Le Diable à Paris*. The 'line of the Midi' refers to the southern side of the boulevards. The course of the Wall of the Farmers-General roughly corresponds to the no. 2 line of the Métro.

50. *Béatrix*, trans. Katharine Prescott Wormeley (Project Gutenberg ebook, 2010), loc. 169532.

51. Staub, like Buisson, was a real person, with a shop on Rue Saint-Marc.

52. *A Woman of Thirty*, loc. 161738 and 161782.

53. *Cousin Bette*, trans. Marion Ayton Crawford (London: Penguin, 1965), pp. 60–1.

54. *A Harlot High and Low*, p. 34. The Butte aux Moulins was flattened in the course of the great works of terracing for the cutting of Avenue de l'Opéra; Rue de Langlade disappeared with it.

55. *Ferragus*, loc. 175100. Rue Pagevin and Rue de Soly disappeared with the cutting of Rue du Louvre and Rue Étienne-Marcel.

56. These numbers still exist, more or less legible.

57. *The Wild Ass's Skin*, pp. 25 and 27.

58. *Old Man Goriot*, pp. 130–1.

59. Edmond Werdet, *Portrait intime de Balzac* (Paris: Le Dentu, 1859), pp. 294–5. The book is mediocre and the anecdotes like this one rather dubious.

60. *L'Almanach des gourmets*, quoted in H. Clouzot and R. H. Valensi, *Le Paris de la Comédie humaine. Balzac et ses fournisseurs* (Paris: Le Goupy, 1926), p. 112.

61. *Lost Illusions*, p. 167. He had been abandoned by Madame de Bargeton, who had brought him to Paris.

62. *The Rise and Fall of César Birotteau*, trans. Katharine Prescott Wormeley (Project Gutenberg ebook, 2010), loc. 155805. This is, unless I am mistaken, the only mention in *The Human Comedy* of a place on the Île Saint-Louis.

63. *The Black Sheep*, p. 56.

64. *Lost Illusions*, pp. 261–2.

65. *A Daughter of Eve*, loc. 62899.

66. This was the royalist insurrection of 13 Vendémaire in Year 4 (5 October 1795), put down on the steps of the Saint-Roch church by artillery set up by a twenty-four-year-old general, Napoléon Bonaparte.

67. Chevet was a real person, the greatest restaurateur of his day, often mentioned in *The Human Comedy*. His premises were in the Palais-Royal. When Lucien de Rubempré invites his friends to his home with Coralie, 'the splendid couvert, the candelabras full of forty candles, the royal offerings of the dessert' came from Chevet. Balzac was a frequent customer of his.

68. *The Rise and Fall of César Birotteau*, loc. 157666–7. General Foy was a liberal deputy, the Champ d'Asile a colony in Texas founded in 1819 by Bonapartist officers.

69. Ibid., loc. 156685ff.

70. Ibid., loc. 157306.

71. Ibid., loc. 156602.

72. *A Harlot High and Low*, p. 117. This was also where we meet old Canquoëlle, a disguise of the formidable spy Peyrade.

73. Gérard de Nerval, *Les Nuits d'octobre* (1852), in *Oeuvres* (Paris: Garnier 1983), p. 419.

74. *Cousin Pons*, p. 59. Rue de Normandie is in the Mont-de-Piété-du-Temple quarter, which can be considered as an extension of the Marais *stricto sensu*.

75. *A Second Home*, trans. Clara Bell (Project Gutenberg ebook, 2010), loc. 120546. Rue Neuve-Saint-François ran between Rue Vieille-du-Temple and Rue Saint-Louis (de Turenne), roughly on the present route of Rue Debelleyme.

76. *Histoire et physiologie des boulevards de Paris*, p. 54. These two establishments were located on Boulevard du Temple, near the end of Rue Charlot.

77. Louis-Sébastien Mercier, *Tableau de Paris*, p. 74.

78. Victor Hugo, *The History of a Crime* (CreateSpace, 2016), p. 22.

79. The quotations without references that follow are taken from this text.

80. *Béatrix*, loc. 169828.

81. The Opéra was established on Rue Le Peletier after the hall on Rue de Richelieu (now the site of Square Louboix) was demolished, a decision made in the wake of the assassination of the Duc de Berry in 1820. The later Opéra Garnier was inaugurated in 1875.

82. The Passage de l'Opéra, with its three arcades, the Baromètre, the Thermomètre and the Horloge, was demolished for the extension of Boulevard Haussmann in the 1920s.

83. *Histoire et physiologie des boulevards de Paris*.

84. Ibid.

85. These were created under Louis XIV, following the lines of the wall of Charles V.

86. The Hôtel d'Évreux subsequently became the property of the financier Beaujon, later of the Duchesse de Bourbon (then known as Élysée-Bourbon). After the Revolution, it passed from one owner to another, until becoming in 1874 the residence of the president of the Republic.

87. *The Wild Ass's Skin*, p. 126.

88. *Correspondance* IV, p. 564. It was in this article in the *Revue Parisienne* that Balzac noted the resemblance, but as Pierrot makes clear, Stendhal maintained that he had never seen the countess.

89. Hôtel de Brunoy was on the site that is now 45 Rue du Faubourg-Saint-Honoré.

90. *Lettres à Madame Hanska*, vol. 1, p. 24.

91. See Rose Fortassier, *Les Mondains de la Comédie humaine* (Paris: Klincksieck, 1974), p. 83.

92. *A Second Home*, loc. 30636.

93. *Old Man Goriot*, p. 127.

94. *The Duchesse de Langeais*, p. 391.

95. *Old Man Goriot*, p. 75. Madame de Restaud 'has been adopted, presented' (in the Faubourg Saint-Germain).

96. Rue Taitbout was then shorter than it is now, extended by Rue du Houssaye and Rue des Trois-Frères.

97. *The Wild Ass's Skin*, pp. 56–7.

98. *A Second Home*, loc. 120175.

99. The Square d'Orléans is a vestige of the splendour of the Chausée-d'Antin, at 80 Rue Taibout.

100. 'Some French Caricaturists', in Charles Baudelaire, *The Mirror of Art* (London: Forgotten Books, 2017), p. 174. Henri Lemaire, editor of Baudelaire's *Curiosités esthétiques*. *L'Art romantique* (Paris: Garnier 1999), explains that the word '*lorette*' was actually coined by Nestor Roqueplan, a journalist and theatre buff.

101. In *Béatrix*. At this time, Paris still had only twelve arrondissements.

102. *A Daughter of Eve*, loc. 63047.

103. In *The Duchesse de Langeais, Lost Illusions, The Wild Ass's Skin, Béatrix, A Daughter of Eve*.

104. *A Daughter of Eve*, loc. 62968.

105. On Esther, who 'came from this cradle of the human species, the homeland of beauty; her mother was Jewish' (her father was Gobseck). *A Harlot High and Low*, p. 51.

106. *Lost Illusions*, p. 432.

107. *Cousin Bette*, pp. 366–7 and 365.

108. Gautier, *Balzac*, p. 93.

109. *Béatrix*, loc. 169525. The Boulevard Extérieur followed the course of the Wall of the Farmers-General.

110. Eugène Sue, *Les Mystères de Paris*, part 4, chapter 6.

111. *Histoire et physiologie des boulevards de Paris*.

112. *The Secrets of the Princesse de Cadignan*, trans. Katharine Prescott Wormeley (Project Gutenberg ebook, 2010), loc. 22415.

113. Ibid., loc. 22475.
114. Ibid., loc. 169024 and 169068.
115. *Lost Illusions*, pp. 183-4.
116. Eugène Sue, *Les Mystères de Paris*, p. 73.
117. François Gasnault, *Guinguettes et lorettes, bals publics à Paris au xixe siècle* (Paris: Aubier, 1986), p. 197.
118. *Cousin Bette*, p. 345.
119. *Histoire et physiologie des boulevards de Paris*, p. 55.

The Press

1. The great book on this subject is that by Roland Chollet, *Balzac journaliste, le tournant de 1830* (Paris: Garnier, 2016 (1983)). The following details are taken from this work.
2. The crisis spared educational and classical publishers, as the Guizot law of 1833 obliged each commune of more than 500 inhabitants to open a school (for boys). Textbooks were bought by the state. Between 1832 and 1834, Louis Hachette sold one million copies of *L'Alphabet et premier livre de lecture*, and hundreds of thousands of arithmetic books. His competitors – Delalain, Renouard, and Dupont – also took advantage of the windfall (J.-Y. Mollier, personal communication). See, by the same author, *Une Autre Histoire de l'édition française* (Paris: La Fabrique, 2015).
3. *Lettres à Madame Hanska*, vol. 1, p. 522.
4. *Correspondance* I, p. 412.
5. *Lost Illusions*, pp. 245–6.
6. *Correspondance* I, p. 317.
7. *Correspondance* V, p. 60
8. Cited in R. Chollet, *Balzac journaliste*, p. 309.
9. This web has been admirably unravelled in Chollet's *Balzac journaliste*.
10. Honoré de Balzac, *Oeuvres diverses* (Paris: Gallimard, 1996), vol. II, pp. 666–7.
11. Ibid., p. 720.
12. Heinrich Heine, *De la France* (Paris: Gallimard, 1994).

13. R. Chollet, *Balzac journaliste*, p. 549. Loève-Veimars was a translator and historian, responsible for diplomatic missions in Russia.

14. *L'Historique du procès du Lys dans la vallée*, in *La Comédie humaine* (Paris: Gallimard 1981), vol. XI, pp. 955–6. By 'justification' Balzac means the length of the lines.

15. *Correspondance* II, p. 92.

16. Ibid., p. 786, note 3.

17. Ibid., p. 785.

18. Balzac gives a lengthy account of the affair in *L'Historique du process auquel a donné lieu le Lys dans la vallée*, which initially appeared in *La Chronique de Paris*.

19. *Correspondance* IV, p. 149, note 1. Dutacq was the founder of *Le Siècle* and the proprietor of the Théâtre du Vaudeville.

20. Balzac, *Études sur M. Beyle* (Geneva: Skira, 1943).

21. Ibid., p. 75.

22. This suggestion was made by Fortassier, *Les Mondaines de la Comédie humaine*, p. 101.

23. *Correspondance* III, p. 586. Stendhal took great account of Balzac's criticisms and was preparing a new edition of *La Chartreuse de Parme* that would have incorporated many of these when he suddenly died.

24. Quotations from Marcel Proust, *By Way of Sainte-Beuve* (London: Hogarth Press, 1984). In the chapter 'Sainte-Beuve and Balzac', it is curious to see Proust taking up the same reproach of 'vulgarity' that his mother had made of Balzac.

25. The two men had planned to establish a single journal together, but finding themselves unable to agree, they each launched their own. Competition between the two would be fierce.

26. *Correspondance* II, p. 482. This would not be the last time. In 1847, Girardin wrote to Balzac, who, tired and ill, had been unable to finish *The Peasants*: 'You are intolerable . . . and if I did not have a certain debt still to settle, I would certainly not publish *The Peasants*, not having had its conclusion' (*Correspondance* V, p. 235).

27. *Correspondance* III, p. 149.

28. Gautier, *Balzac*, p. 84. In *Une Autre Histoire de l'édition française*, J.-Y. Mollier remarks that the publication of novels in serial form helped

Belgian counterfeiting; they only had to typeset the text as issues arrived, and bring out the volume the same day that the final episode appeared.

29. *Correspondance* III, p. 192. This refers to the first part of *A Harlot High and Low*.
30. Ibid., p. 297, 31 May 1837.
31. In 'Madame Bovary par Gustave Flaubert', published in *L'Artiste*, 18 October 1857.
32. *Revue de Paris*, 28 December 1844. Cited in *Correspondance* V, p. 42, note 1.
33. Letter to Laurent-Jan, *Correspondance* V, p. 488.
34. Honoré de Balzac, *Oeuvres diverses*, vol. II, p. 1223; 22 August 1833.
35. This *Monographie* was published in 1843 in *La Grande Ville, nouveau tableau de Paris, comique, critique et philosophique*, a collective work whose other authors included Alexandre Dumas and Frédéric Soulie.
36. *Lost Illusions*, pp. 228–9.
37. Ibid., pp. 249–50.
38. *The Firm of Nucingen*, trans. James Waring (Project Gutenberg ebook, 2010), loc. 13285.

Publishers

1. *Correspondance* II, p. 71. The passage refers to the first proofs of *Louis Lambert*, which Gosselin published.
2. Ibid., pp. 90–1.
3. *Correspondance* IV, p. 208.
4. Some publishers charged Balzac for part of these costs.
5. These were calculated on the print run and not on sales. It is generally estimated that the 1830 franc is equivalent to 2.50 euros in 2023.
6. It is not easy to follow Balzac's works through successive publishers. The large number of titles, the first publication of novels in magazines or serials (almost systematically after *Old Man Goriot*), and the frequent reprints all make it hard to find one's way around. Fortunately, there is a book by Stéphane Vachon, *Les Travaux et les jours*

d'Honoré de Balzac, chronologie de la création balzacienne (Paris: Presses universitaires de Vincennes, 1992), which sheds light on the subject with a year-by-year chronology over 300 pages.

7. *Correspondance* I, p. 289.

8. A facsimile of this catalogue is given by Roger Pierrot in his *Honoré de Balzac*.

9. *Correspondance* II, p. 132.

10. Ibid., p. 141.

11. Roger Pierrot, *Honoré de Balzac*, p. 132, note 2.

12. Mame had sent him the 1,000 francs requested.

13. Ibid., p. 157. The 'adviser' is not clearly identified.

14. Ibid., p. 165.

15. Ibid., p. 318, note.

16. Letter to the Duchesse d'Abrantès, *Correspondance* II, p. 341.

17. *Lettres à Madame Hanska*, vol. I, p. 332. In October 1833, the widow Béchet had signed a contract with Balzac for a series of novels grouped under the title 'Studies of morals in the 19th century'. This contract provided for 27,000 francs in royalties to be paid as the texts were delivered.

18. *Correspondance* II, p. 152.

19. Published in *L'Écho des Théâtres*, 23 August 1846.

20. Baudelaire, 'The Salon of 1846', in *The Mirror of Art* (New York: Doubleday, 1956), p. 130. Alfonso Lavrado Fontanares, aka Quinola, is the title character in Balzac's play *Les Ressources de Quinola*, performed at the Odéon in 1842, which takes place in the Spain of Philip II.

21. Souverain republished the complete works of 'Horace de Saint-Aubin', as well as the first editions of *Pierrette, Pierre Grassou, Ursule Mirouet, A Murky Business*, and *The Black Sheep*.

22. On the Bibliothèque Charpentier Library, see J.-Y. Mollier, *Une Autre Histoire*, pp. 198ff.

23. *Correspondance* IV, p. 313. It was however specified that 'new works will not be included in the present concession until two years after their first sale in volume form, or three years after their publication in newspapers or magazines'.

24. 7 December 1842; *Lettres à Madame Hanska*, vol. II, pp. 132–3.

25. *Correspondance* IV, p. 329 (October 1841). Abbé Troubert and Abbé Birotteau are characters in *The Curé of Tours*; Philippe Bridau in *The Black Sheep*; Gouraud, Vinet, and Mother Lorrain in *Pierrette*. Roguin is the bankrupt notary in *César Birotteau*, and also appears in *Eugénie Grandet*.

26. Ibid., p. 465.

At the Theatre

1. Gautier, *Balzac*, pp. 100–2. The friends in question were Laurent-Jan, Ourliac and Lassailly. The drama was *Vautrin*, and Harel the director of the Théâtre de la Porte Saint-Martin. As Balzac explains in *Old Man Goriot*, 'the recent invention of the *Diorama* . . . had, in some studios, inspired the conceit of ending words in *rama*' (pp. 46–7).

2. Edmond Biré, 'Balzac au théâtre', in *Le Correspondant*, 25 October 1895, pp. 318–51.

3. *Correspondance* V, p. 475 (9 February 1849). Hostein directed in turn the Renaissance, then the Ambigu, then the Théâtre-Historique.

4. With the exception of the Gaîté, where Florine began as an extra. The other theatres on the Boulevard du Crime were the Théâtre-Lyrique, the Cirque-Olympique run by the Franconis, the Funambules, whose star was the mime Deburau, the Délassements-Comiques and the Petit-Lazzari, named after an Italian mime of the tenth century.

5. *Lettres à Madame Hanska*, vol. II, p. 474. Quoted in Linzy Ericka Dickinson, *Theatre in Balzac's La Comédie humaine* (Amsterdam: Rodopi, 2000).

6. *The Secrets of the Princesse de Cadignan*, loc. 22579 ff. The young man in question is the Republican Michel Chrestien.

7. The Théâtre Italien moved from building to building throughout the nineteenth century. At the time of *Old Man Goriot*, in the early 1820s, it was located in the Salle Favart, on the site of the present Opéra Comique.

8. *Old Man Goriot*, p. 114.

9. *A Harlot High and Low*, p. 32. Esther is aware that she is known as the Torpedo, 'the last of these creatures and the most infamous'.

10. *A Daughter of Eve*, loc. 63066 ff.

11. *Lost Illusions*, p. 278. The Panorama-Dramatique had a brief existence, between 1821 and 1823. It had permission for dramas, comedies, and vaudevilles, but with one restriction: there could not be more than two actors or actresses speaking on stage at the same time (Dickinson, *Theatre in Balzac's La Comédie humaine*, p. 39). In the passage quoted, Balzac mixes fictional characters (Vignol, Florine) with real ones (Potier, a famous actor of the time).

12. Ibid., p. 279.

13. Ibid., p. 387.

14. St. Vachon, *Les Travaux et les jours*, pp. 243 and 281.

15. The others were *L'École des ménages*, accepted in 1839 at the Renaissance but replaced at the last moment by Alexandre Dumas's *L'Alchimiste*; *Paméla Giraud*, staged at the Gaîté in 1843; and *La Marâtre*, performed in 1848 at the Théâtre-Historique. To these must be added *Mercadet* (subsequently *Le Faiseur*), which was not performed during Balzac's lifetime but was subsequently revived several times, most recently by the Comédie Française in 1993.

16. *Correspondance* IV, p. 47 (29 February 1840). 'P'osper' must have been a common joke between the two men, for Balzac also signs his letter 'P'osper'.

17. Gozlan, *Balzac en pantoufles*, pp. 56, 59, 60.

18. Quoted in *Correspondance* IV, p. 846.

19. *Lettres à Madame Hanska*, September 1841. *Les Rubriques* would become *Les Ressources*.

20. *Correspondance* IV, p. 355.

21. Gozlan, *Balzac en pantoufles*, pp. 67–9.

22. *Lettres à Madame Hanska*, 8 April 1842.

Friends, Politics, and the 'Realism' of Balzac's Paris

1. The Abbaye-aux-Bois was a Cistercian abbey which offered accommodation to people of quality. It was located on the present

site of Rue Récamier, and destroyed with the cutting of Boulevard Raspail.

2. Marcel Proust, *By Way of Saint-Beuve* (London: Hogarth Press, 1984), p. 151.

3. Quoted in Pierrot, *Honoré de Balzac*, p. 185. Pierrot notes that in *Lost Illusions* (p. 305), Lucien de Rubempré makes a pastiche of this style at the start of his first article ('People come and go, talk and walk, look round for something and find nothing').

4. To whom he respectively dedicated *The Secrets of the Princesse de Cadignan* and *The Memoirs of Two Young Wives*.

5. Gautier, *Balzac*, pp. 4–8.

6. *Lettres à Madame Hanska*, vol. II, pp. 133–4. Hôtel Pimodan on Quai d'Anjou is now the Hôtel Lauzun.

7. Charles Baudelaire, *Artificial Paradises* (New York: Kensington Publishing, 1998), chapter 5, 'Moral'.

8. *Correspondance* III, p. 204, n.d. The 'work' in question is not clearly identified but is thought to be the new edition of *The Unknown Masterpiece*.

9. *Correspondance* V, p. 782 (20 June 1850). In postscript, in Balzac's own hand: 'I can neither read nor write.'

10. George Sand, *Histoire de ma vie*, quoted in Pierrot, *Honoré de Balzac*, p. 180.

11. Quoted in *Correspondance* I, p. 1300, note.

12. Letter to Madame Hanska, quoted in Pierrot, *Honoré de Balzac*, p. 319.

13. 'It was in connection with Liszt and Mme d'Agoult that she gave me the subject of *Les Galériens* or *Les Amours forcés* [the original title of *Béatrix*], which I am going to do, because, in her position, she cannot. Keep this secret well' (letter to Madame Hanska quoted in Pierrot, *Honoré de Balzac*, p. 320).

14. *Béatrix*, loc. 166321. Clara Gazul was a pseudonym of Prosper Merimée.

15. Ibid., loc. 167493 and 168207.

16. *Correspondance* IV, p. 18 (18 January 1840).

17. *Correspondance* V, p. 893; undated. As Chopin writes in the margin of this letter, 'Balzac almost always signed himself Mar in his correspondence with Madame Sand.'

18. *Correspondance* IV, p. 507 (October 1842).

19. *Correspondance* IV, p. 79 (18 March 1840).

20. Ibid., p. 170, letter of thanks for an article in the *Revue Parisienne* on *Les Rayons et les ombres*: 'M. Hugo is certainly the greatest poet of the nineteenth century.'

21. Ibid, p. 780 (20 February 1845). Hugo lived on Place Royale [now Place des Vosges] which was a good walk from Passy.

22. The scene clearly takes place in Balzac's house on Rue Fortunée. The bust was by David d'Angers.

23. *Correspondance* IV, p. 70 (14 March 1840).

24. Quoted in *Correspondance* IV, p. 293, note 1.

25. *The Seamy Side of History*, trans. Katharine Prescott Wormeley (Project Gutenberg ebook, 2010), loc. 170323.

26. *Lost Illusions*, p. 221.

27. With one exception, in *The Secrets of the Princesse de Cadignan* (loc. 22591): 'The prince, as you know' – the princess tells Madame d'Espard – 'defended the Tuileries on the riverside, during the July days . . . "I came near being killed at four o'clock," he told me. "I was aimed at by one of the insurgents, when a young man, with a long beard, whom I have often seen the opera, and who was leading the attack, threw up the man's gun, and saved me." ' The young man in question was Michel Chrestien, who had prevented the death of the husband of the woman he loved, a death that others would have welcomed.

28. *Correspondance* I, p. 303 (21 July 1830).

29. *The Wild Ass's Skin*, pp. 57–8.

30. *The Duchesse de Langeais*, p. 348.

31. *A Daughter of Eve*, loc. 62374.

32. *Correspondance* I, p. 315 (6 November 1830); *Correspondance* II, p. 258 (1 March 1833).

33. See above, p. 55.

34. *The Chouans*, trans. Katharine Prescott Wormeley (Project Gutenberg, 2010), loc. 147532. We come across Marshal Hulot again, a little senile but still dignified, in *Cousin Bette*, where his brother, Baron Hulot, is a major – though disrespectable – character.

35. 'The Duchesse de Langeais', pp. 305–8.
36. *Béatrix*, loc. 169691.
37. He would eventually stand as a candidate, in 1849, and receive just some twenty votes.
38. *Correspondance* IV, p. 636 (14 December 1843). The deed was not concluded, perhaps because of Balzac's financial demands.
39. Ibid., p. 178. Roger Pierrot, *Honoré de Balzac*, quotes in a note what Balzac wrote in the *Revue Parisienne*: 'Like all the great innovators, like Jesus, Fourier broke with the past of the world. According to him, the social environment in which they move makes passions alone subversive. He conceived the colossal work of appropriating environments to passions, of breaking down obstacles, of preventing struggles.'
40. *Facino Cane*, pp. 3–5.
41. *Ferragus*, loc. 90652. There are many female workers in *The Human Comedy*, such as Ida, Ferragus's mistress, a corset maker, but they are home workers, not workers in the emerging factories.
42. It is not a question of dates. *Béatrix* appeared in 1844, and the action takes place over a long period that goes beyond the appearance of the railway.
43. *A Start in Life*, trans. Katharine Prescott Wormeley (Project Gutenberg ebook, 2010), loc. 37976.
44. These communes were officially annexed in 1860.
45. Cited in Jeannine Guichardet, *Balzac archéologue de Paris*, p. 30.
46. Or almost nothing: a brief allusion, in *Cousin Bette*, when the Prince de Wissembourg says to Victorien Hulot: 'We want to appoint you as legal adviser to the War Office, which on the engineering side has more litigation than it can deal with, arising from the plans for the Paris fortifications' (p. 349).
47. Baudelaire, 'Théophile Gautier', in *Curiosités esthetiques*.
48. *Ferragus*, loc. 90587.
49. Baudelaire, 'Théophile Gautier', in *Curiosités esthétiques*.
50. At the start of *Ferragus*, loc. 90599.
51. *Le Mendiant*.

Index of Names

Fictional characters in *italics*

Index of Places

Index of Works